the British art show

OLD ALLEGIANCES AND NEW DIRECTIONS 1979–1984

Published for the
Arts Council of Great Britain by
ORBIS · LONDON

EXHIBITION ORGANIZERS:
NICOLA BENNETT (SELECTION), ROGER MALBERT (TOUR)

EXHIBITION ASSISTANT:
LISE CONNELLAN

CATALOGUE EDITOR:
NICOLA BENNETT

EDUCATION ADVISER:
HELEN LUCKETT

PERFORMANCE, FILM AND VIDEO COORDINATOR:
ROGER MALBERT

CATALOGUE DESIGN:
GRAHAM DAVIS ASSOCIATES

COLOUR SEPARATIONS:
MULLIS MORGAN LIMITED

First published in Great Britain by Orbis
Publishing Limited, London, for the Arts
Council of Great Britain 1984

Filmset by SX Composing Limited
Printed in Great Britain by BAS Printers Limited

Orbis ISBN Hardback 0-85613-792-8
Orbis ISBN Paperback 0-85613-794-4
Arts Council ISBN Hardback 0-7287-0425-0
Arts Council ISBN Paperback 0-7287-0426-9

THE
BRITISH
ART
SHOW

OLD ALLEGIANCES AND NEW DIRECTIONS 1979–1984

An Arts Council touring exhibition

BIRMINGHAM
City of Birmingham Museum and Art Gallery
and Ikon Gallery
2 November – 22 December 1984

EDINBURGH
Royal Scottish Academy
19 January – 24 February 1985

SHEFFIELD
Mappin Art Gallery
16 March – 4 May 1985

SOUTHAMPTON
Southampton Art Gallery
18 May – 30 June 1985

CONTENTS

List of artists

The following artists have been selected by:
MARJORIE ALLTHORPE-GUYTON, ALEXANDER MOFFAT and JON THOMPSON

ART & LANGUAGE
KEVIN ATHERTON
TERRY ATKINSON
FRANK AUERBACH
GILLIAN AYRES

JO BAER AND BRUCE ROBBINS
PETER BAILEY
BASIL BEATTIE
JOHN BELLANY
TONY BEVAN
STUART BRISLEY
VICTOR BURGIN
PAUL BUSH

STEVEN CAMPBELL
ANTHONY CARO
JOHN CARTER
TONY CARTER
HELEN CHADWICK
MARC CHAIMOWICZ
ALAN CHARLTON
TONY CRAGG
MICHAEL CRAIG-MARTIN

JOHN DAVIES
RICHARD DEACON
GRAHAM DURWARD

IAN HAMILTON FINLAY
ROSE FINN-KELCEY
GARETH FISHER
JOEL FISHER
BARRY FLANAGAN

GILBERT & GEORGE
SANDRA GOLDBACHER
ANTONY GORMLEY

MICK HARTNEY
TIM HEAD
GERARD HEMSWORTH
SUSAN HILLER
JOHN HILLIARD
HOWARD HODGKIN
SHIRAZEH HOUSHIARY
ANTHONY HOWELL
JOHN HOYLAND
JOHN HYATT

STEPHEN JOHNSON
PETER JOSEPH

ANISH KAPOOR
MARY KELLY
KEN KIFF
R. B. KITAJ
LEON KOSSOFF

BOB LAW	PAULA REGO
RICHARD LONG	
	MICHAEL SANDLE
LEONARD McCOMB	TERRY SETCH
JOCK McFADYEN	JOHN SMITH
IAN McKEEVER	RAY SMITH
STEPHEN McKENNA	STATION HOUSE OPERA
BRUCE McLEAN	
ALASTAIR MacLENNAN	ANDREW WALKER
KENNETH MARTIN	JOHN WALKER
JOHN MURPHY	BOYD WEBB
	RICHARD WENTWORTH
AVIS NEWMAN	ALISON WILDING
GERALD NEWMAN	VICTOR WILLING·
PHILIP NICOL	ADRIAN WISZNIEWSKI
	BILL WOODROW
THÉRÈSE OULTON	STEPHEN TAYLOR WOODROW
JAYNE PARKER	JOHN YEADON

PREFACE

In 1979 the Arts Council presented 'The British Art Show', a large-scale exhibition of 112 artists selected by the artist and critic William Packer. It was the biggest exhibition ever toured by the Arts Council and visited three cities – Sheffield, Newcastle and Bristol – to be seen by over 77,000 people. From the outset we intended to organize such exhibitions periodically and in 1982 we invited Marjorie Allthorpe-Guyton, Alexander Moffat and Jon Thompson to work together on a second 'British Art Show'. Like their predecessor they were asked to choose the work they considered the most interesting, this time of 80 artists.

As we have done with our Hayward Annuals, we decided to vary the format for the second 'British Art Show'. We wanted to retain the element of personal choice but to present a structured and argued view of the 'best' in British art from 1979 to 1984. The contradiction implicit in basing the selection both on objective analysis and subjective judgment was not the only one in the brief which called for reconciliation. The thoroughness of the selection procedure allowed the exhibition the scope of a fully representative survey, yet the conclusion was to be an interpretative summary. While the ground was to be worked in detail, it was to be viewed overall from an historical perspective. The means may have been necessary for the ends, but it was obviously more than we could ask of a single human being. We therefore decided to look for three selectors whose combined knowledge and interests would produce a broadly-based view. And – another impossible contradiction – it was essential that they work together compatibly through two years of selection.

Eighty-two artists and artists' groups are included in this exhibition, a selection which includes performance, film and video art and work using photography and mixed media as well as painting and sculpture. To select such an exhibition is an opportunity but it is also a responsibility. In this case, it meant two years of visiting artists and galleries all over Britain. The selectors considered the work of 1000 artists, a fact which speaks for their dedication. As for what they brought to the process of looking at work, this is perhaps indicated by the large number of artists who said how much they valued their visits. To attempt a selection which does not sacrifice conviction for convenience, nor coherence for partiality demands the careful balancing of personal response and objective argument, and our thanks go to the selectors who generously committed so much time and thought to the selection of the exhibition and to the writing of the catalogue.

Marjorie Allthorpe-Guyton was Assistant Keeper of Art at Norwich Castle Museum until 1979. Her practical gallery and exhibition experience, her involvement in the work of two contemporary art societies, and her open-minded interest in the visual arts were among the qualities that recommended her. Alexander Moffat is a Scottish figurative painter perhaps best known for his portraits: 'Seven Poets', an exhibition of portraits of Scottish poets, toured the UK from 1980 to 1983 and the Scottish National Portrait Gallery commissioned him to paint the novelist Muriel Spark this year. Not surprisingly his first allegiance is to figurative painting, although, as Chairman of the New 57 Gallery in Edinburgh from 1969 to 1978 and as tutor at Glasgow School of Art, his knowledge of the visual arts is based on wide experience. Jon Thompson has long been fascinated by art theory and his work as an artist reflects this interest in the language and ideas of art. He was Dean of the School of Fine Art at Goldsmiths' College from 1970 to 1980 and is now Director of their Post-Graduate Studies course.

The selection of 'The British Art Show' was an evolutionary process with ideas and expectations being adapted as the focus gradually became clear. One of the aims was a discussion of the 'state of the art' (to quote the title of Tim Head's work in the show), and for the selectors this meant mainstream developments. Thus their interest has been in artists whose work, in their view, contributes to this debate. Many of them work and/or show in London, but it is interesting to note that 43 of the artists now living in London were born and grew up elsewhere.

The subtitle 'Old Allegiances and New Directions' is an indication of diversity. The fissure which has broken up the surface of contemporary art most radically is the challenge to Modernism – the progressive tradition of formal innovation which has dominated art practice for most of this century – by a return to traditional techniques and representational imagery. It is a theme of the catalogue and does not need to be discussed again here, but there are implications for an exhibition which sets out to interpret a period just as that challenge starts to make itself felt. While the selection includes figurative painting, it also comprises artists who are still working vigorously within Abstract traditions and others who are developing ideas and practices which started with the conceptualism of the sixties and seventies. It features photography, film and video – untraditional media. Against expectations, the selectors found little authentic painting of the 'new expressionist' kind, which has been at the forefront of the 'new art' in Europe and America. Art in Britain has not been taken over, simply stirred up.

The implications of a move from Modernism are far-reaching for people who look at art, as well as for artists. If art is no longer primarily about itself, if artists are using representational imagery which can be understood in terms of recognition and association, then it no longer demands the specialist knowledge that Abstraction has, unfortunately, appeared to require. The new use of imagery has allowed artists to treat subjects which had become the territory of other disciplines, such as film and literature, and to engage openly in the issues which concern our society in general.

The selectors have arranged and written about the show in groupings which focus on certain concerns which they see as linking artists in illuminating and not necessarily expected ways. The groups are intended as one starting point to open the exhibition to individual interpretation; they are not fixed categories.

The selectors join us in thanking all those who have made this exhibition possible. First, we acknowledge the artists who by taking part in 'The British Art Show' *are* 'The British Art Show'. We are very grateful to them and to all the artists who showed generous help and hospitality at all stages of the selection process. We would also like to thank those to whom we went for suggestions and advice – artists, dealers, collectors, our colleagues in the Regional Arts Associations, in the Scottish and Welsh Arts Councils and in the Arts Council of Northern Ireland – and those who have kindly lent to the exhibition.

Putting on a touring exhibition of this size stretches our own resources to the full and would not be possible without the participation of the galleries in which it is shown. We are grateful to the staff of the galleries for their collaboration, and to the Scottish Arts Council, who are responsible for the showing of the exhibition in Edinburgh.

We appreciate the support 'The British Art Show' has received from several sources. We are particularly grateful to Citibank for their generous sponsorship of the Birmingham and Edinburgh showings. The joint publication of this catalogue with Orbis Publishing Ltd, involving the collaboration of Mullis Morgan Ltd, has made possible a more substantial publication than would otherwise have been the case. A printed exhibition guide is being made available thanks to sponsorship from The British Petroleum Company plc, the support of The Baring Foundation has allowed us to appoint a guide-lecturer at each venue, and Chromacopy have made and donated the photographic display prints used in the exhibition.

JOANNA DREW
DIRECTOR OF ART

NICOLA BENNETT
EXHIBITION ORGANIZER

REVERSING
THE
TRANS-ATLANTIC
DRIFT

JON THOMPSON

When you see what the Abstractionists have done since 1940, it's worse than ever, optical. They're really up to their eyes in the Retina . . . Before, painting had other functions: it could be religious, philosophical, moral . . . It's absolutely ridiculous. It has to change; it hasn't always been like this.
(Marcel Duchamp)[1]

Following the decline of French painting in the late forties and early fifties, artists, critics and dealers from Britain and continental Europe looked to New York for a measure of all that was most vital in the visual arts. With the Venice Biennale of 1980 this state of affairs was suddenly and dramatically over-turned. As one walked through the cool, vaulted spaces of the Castello and the Camera della Salle, and wandered from national pavilion to national pavilion beneath the great plane trees of the Giardino, it was the European artists who captured the imagination. European veterans such as Brood-thaers, Hesse, Beuys, Fabro, Merz and Kounellis held stately watch over a new and eager generation of artists: the Germans – Baselitz, Kiefer, Penck, Immendorff, Lüpertz and Polke – and the Italians – Chia, Clemente, Poulini, Cucci and Paladino. By comparison, and with one or two notable exceptions – Serra perhaps, Lee-Byars, Thek and Jenny – the Americans looked staid and academic, preoccupied with narrow formal and technical questions.

But the impression given by Venice 1980 – of the American art world in decline – was to a degree illusory. New York was still a hyper-active centre of both practice and patronage, and its capacity to generate and sustain innovation, within its own terms of reference, was undiminished. We were not, then, seeing another Paris in its twilight years: tired, complacent and inward-looking, its power slipping away unheeded, but one of these moments in

Francesco Clemente
No. 1 of 12
paintings from
THE MIDNIGHT SUN
1982
Anthony d'Offay Gallery,
London

history when a ruling elite is challenged by those whom it had believed to be secure, happy and docile subjects. America's cultural empire was in revolt. The artists of Germany and Italy, waving a critical, even an accusatory finger at the 'internationalist' philosophy which was at the heart of modern American art, were on the move and were poised to conquer New York.

In the same exhibition, the British contingent was typically idiosyncratic. It appeared, for the most part, to be staying coyly to one side of the main conflict. Artists such as Kenneth Martin and Leonard McComb were never much taken with American art and continued to see their lineage (in common with many of the older generation of British artists) as stemming directly from Cézanne and the post-Impressionists, distant sources of Modernism. Only Cragg, McLean and Head seemed pertinent to the main argument. As for the middle-generation artists back at home, it was hard to think of more than a handful who could have made a vital contribution to either side, and who would not have appeared eccentric or mere shadows of the main protagonists. All in all it pointed to the curious marginality of British art in the international art world at the beginning of the eighties.

Two years later, the art cognoscenti assembled at the 1982 Biennale proclaimed Cragg, Flanagan, Woodrow, Vilmouth, Blacker, Cox, Gormley and Kapoor the most vital and coherent national school of sculpture (if school is not too misleading a term) currently at work. In this instance, unusually, their perception of a change in British art was neither a momentary aberration nor merely the result of collective amnesia. On the contrary, they brought to public attention the first fruits, albeit imperfect, of a profound shift in British art practice not dissimilar to that which had occurred in German and Italian painting. Among the younger generation of British artists, this change of perspective had been under

Sigmar Polke
SKELETT/SKELETON
1974
Saatchi Collection, London

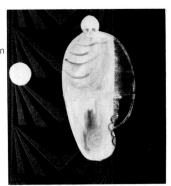

way for some time, showing itself as a loosening of the bonds which tied them to American ways of thinking about and making art.

Changes of the kind which surfaced in the Venice Biennale in 1980 and in 1982 seldom, if ever, take place in isolation. They have their roots in economic, social and political realities and in the shifting sands of contemporary thought on a wide range of topics. And in the modern world details must always be placed in a global context. We must look then to international affairs if we are properly to understand the changes taking place on our own doorstep.

International affairs since the Second World War have been dominated by the division between East and West, and political allegiance to either side has demanded a high degree of cultural alignment. In the case of the 'Iron Curtain countries', submission to the state's view of what is ideologically correct and therefore permissible in arts and letters led to the wide-spread suppression of artists and their works. In the West, Roosevelt, with the WPA programmes of the Depression years,[2] successfully forged a link between artistic and social freedom. Paradoxically, the result of both strategies was cultural imperialism, requiring the suppression of local identities, sensibilities and aspirations in favour of priorities formulated at the centre. In the West, of course, the system functions on a much longer leash, allowing dissidence to flourish as part of a continuous flow of change and counter-change, but it is designed to achieve maximum absorption no matter how difficult digestion might be. This process depends crucially on economic power, which America, despite the drain placed on its resources by its mistaken military intervention in South-east Asia, was able to sustain until the first oil crisis of the seventies. It was this sense of economic superiority and the overwhelming national self-confidence it bred, that enabled the USA to launch its 'cultural colonization' of Britain and continental Europe.

The Yalta Conference in 1945 made America supreme in an alliance of nations whose allegiance it held by simply ministering to their very great material needs. But some of these countries – Britain, Italy and France in particular – displayed dangerous tendencies towards independent and possibly destabilizing political thought and action, and this at the forefront of America's defences against proselytizing communism. Something had to be done to shore up the political ideology of the West. In the words of Stephen Spender, 'the battle was on for the mind of Europe'.[3]

That America should choose to use cultural colonization, and that the new painting became a key instrument for penetrating the European consciousness, might be thought to be one of the more curious facts of modern history. But it is, perhaps, not so curious when viewed against the background of America's own internal political struggles. After the traumas of the Great Depression and later of the McCarthy purges, it had successfully 'liberalized' its intelligentsia and depoliticized its artists, isolating extremists on both right and left. The centrist mainstream of American domestic politics not only prevailed, but emerged immensely strengthened. It is hardly surprising, therefore, that America should apply this model to achieve a similar stabilizing miracle here in Europe.

Curiously enough, the process was exemplified by the art critic Clement Greenberg, who provided the critique of 'high formalism' whereby America took on the mantle of the avant-garde.[4] His lateral progress from the anti-Stalinist left to the liberal centre is clearly charted in his writings from 1930 on. His was not, of course, the only voice raised in support of the new painting with its liberal democratic values. By the mid-fifties any howls of abuse had been drowned by eulogies of praise from the president and key politicians. American art had achieved official recognition; henceforth it might be used by politicians for political ends.

The Eisenhower Administration flooded Europe with exhibitions designed to demonstrate the vitality of American culture and to promote, subliminally, the efficacy of the American way of life. Among the European countries, Britain was hardest hit by the American invasion. Not only did Britain share common bonds with America out of her mercantile past, but more importantly, they shared a common tongue. It was comparatively easy, therefore, and required no conspiratorial effort on their part, for the pundits of American art theory – Rosenberg, Greenberg, Ashton and Fried – to gain influence with English critics and through them effect in the British art press a full rehearsal of the values exemplified by the new American painting. Significantly, the influx of American ideas coincided with Coldstream's restructuring of the British art schools.[5]

The great tradition of British art education, founded principally by Ruskin and Morris in the nineteenth century, was shattered by two world wars. The schools were left high and dry on a sandbank of passé convictions, without real direction or purpose. Social Realism flowered briefly in one or two London Schools in the fifties but had failed to establish itself as the mainstream; the flirtation with French painting continued, but in a fitful, half-hearted fashion, filtered and homogenized by earlier British interpreters of Paris. The early sixties found the art schools ripe for revolution.

Coldstream's approach to his task was essentially a reformist one, but this was not true of many who were called upon to implement his programme — they cherished more radical objectives. For them the development of modernist attitudes was the central purpose of the education process. The student population, whose to-ing and fro-ing between London and New York had been steadily increasing, made similar demands, and this proved to be an irresistible combination. Within a period of three years, a system of teaching, based on traditional techniques of drawing and picture-making which had been central to British art teaching for almost a century, was dissolved. Those who were not prepared to undergo an instant conversion were swept unceremoniously to one side and replaced by a band of young, recently graduated teachers, most of whom espoused the American idiom.

Of course it would be foolish to argue that the schools would have done better to stay as they were, or even that all the changes that took place were necessarily bad. It is important to recognize, however, that this process was not a matter of re-invigorating a secure visual culture by drawing within its purview aesthetic values from another, perhaps more exotic, culture. It was not, for instance, comparable to the Japanese influence on French painting in the second half of the nineteenth century, or to the influence of tribal African sculpture on early Cubism. With traditions already weakened, British art education and through it British art was vulnerable to an American influence which was more of a usurpation than a fertilization, requiring redefinitions of the most fundamental kind.

The American modernist's vision of the creative project is, in essence, a deeply materialistic one; 'the product', as the Italian critic, Bonito Oliva, puts it, 'of a highly competitive merchandizing society'.[6] As a broad aesthetic philosophy it focuses on the process of manufacture, on the exploration of material properties and their experimental application. It makes no distinction between the instruments of expression and what is expressed. The pursuit of 'object quality' leads to the dissolving of figure into field, the demotion of representation in favour of 'presentation', and the celebration of the coincidence of surface and image. Abstraction, couched in these terms, conceives of the 'art object' in a very particular way — as autonomous and self-referencing, the maker and exemplifier of its own rule-book, denying conspicuous content and celebrating its independence and its irresponsibility. By the same token, it ignores the hidden domain of ideology, tradition and history which are fundamental to European culture. This kind of self-referential art puts the emphasis on confrontation, on the immediate response, which must in turn transform the conception of art history. In this context art history is seen in a linear way, as a continuous process of action and reaction, and tradition is seen as a succession of distinct creative moments. These are the twin founding concepts which Rosenberg[7] dubbed 'The Tradition of the New', and they are the immature offspring of a new culture.

Politically speaking, this view of tradition and history incorporates a liberal utopian idea of progress: the idea that — given that human individuals have the opportunity to achieve material security coupled with freedom — human affairs 'progress' quite naturally onwards and upwards towards a platonic ideal of 'the good'. Such a view begs what are for Europeans inescapable questions which might broadly be said to subsist in the spiritual domain — of good and evil, love and hatred, life and death, heaven and hell. To the European mind these are ideological givens, and 'the good' therefore has to be forged out of the struggle against the negative forces at play in the world and in the human heart. It is this that gives rise to the aesthetic impulse, and the 'sublime moment' and 'the dark night of the soul' are thus the poles around which revolves the rich pattern of European art. This troublesome spirituality is a monument to human perversity as well as to human aspiration, and is conspicuously absent from the vast bulk of American post-war art. Presumably it was lost in the pursuit of 'object quality', part of that reduction which Duchamp called 'retinal', the art object reduced to the status of all other objects in the world.

When Duchamp pleads, then, for an art which is not 'retinal', but which is religious, philosophical or moral, he is acknowledging his European origins and setting himself aside from the art of his adopted country.[8] His definition of 'retinal' art begins in Europe with Courbet, but reaches its apotheosis in America with Abstract Expressionism and Minimal Art. In this he makes the same journey as Greenberg and Fried. For him, though, it is the charting of a decline; for them, it is proof positive that America has successfully shouldered the burden of what they (mistakenly) take as European tradition. But the connections which they so carefully plotted, between Pollock and late Monet, for example, or between Louis and Matisse, seem to us now to be tenuous and ill-conceived. We only have to set a Pollock alongside a Monet, and a Louis alongside a Matisse and these connections are reduced before our eyes to mere material, formal and stylistic similarities. They ignore the impulses which caused Monet to build for himself Proust's 'garden of reverie' before painting it, or Matisse imprisoned in his wheelchair, to cut and to tear his great and moving representations of an earthly paradise. Comparisons of this kind are perhaps unfair to Pollock and Louis, but they do exemplify the 'reductive' tendency which bedevils American aesthetics: the tendency which never fails to invoke the tautology that 'the thing itself' – its material and formal properties – are both the object and the significance of the object. It is this curious aesthetic reduction which, until the beginning of the 1930s, drove American artists to pursue greater and greater degrees of conceptual elegance; it drove American art into a downward spiral leading to the death of art itself.

Perhaps the most common critical cliché is that which refers to British art as essentially 'literary'. During the period of 'high modernism', it was also the most common term of critical abuse. Used to close-off questions about content and subject matter, it signified that a work was not, in the modernist sense, self-contained – that it was compromised by extraneous material drawn from a quite separate domain of experience. Philosophically, such a separation is untenable; historically, as we have seen, it goes against the whole tradition of European art from the cave painters to artists of the present day. The term 'literary' is indeed applicable to British art, as it is to the art of any country which possesses an 'old' culture, wherein the history of visual art is inextricably bound up with the history of literature. And at the centre of the knot is the poetic imagination. European culture cannot escape from the distant echoes of ancient tales passed on by word of mouth, whether declaimed, spoken or sung; tales which tell of human passion, desire and action, and place them within reach of earthly and divine retribution. The poetic voice sounds across the chasm which exists between primordial nature and contemporary culture; between universal experience and experience as it is expresed through individual human temperament. It is both vision and colour. Just as the literary device of metaphor depends on visual experience, so it is, as the Spanish poet Lorca says, the 'poetic tone that colours the landscape'.[9]

The distinctive 'poetic tone' of British art is most clearly discernible in the pastoral paintings and poems of the eighteenth and nineteenth centuries. Theirs is no arcadia, rather it is the Phrygian fields worked by a long-established serfdom, creatures intimate with the ageless knowledge that nature gives – a knowledge which for the cultured mind is always and forever lost. In Constable, the rustic lad who sleeps beneath the tree is the poet in every man. He has the poet's cap beside him and in his innocence he sleeps; he has neither the desire for

Morris Louis
ALPHA-PHI
1961
The Tate Gallery, London

nor the means of poetic utterance. Such a metaphor reveals to us the 'poetic tone' of the British vision: fixed upon nature it is powered by a sense of loss and as a result is tainted with irrational fear.

How different the American view of nature. A telling statement about the relationship between the natural world and American formal Abstraction was made by the American art critic E. C. Goossen in his introduction to the Arts Council's 'The Art of the Real',[10] a seminal exhibition of American art mounted at the Tate Gallery in 1968. He says, 'the new work of art is very much like a chunk of nature, a rock, a tree, a cloud, and possesses much the same hermetic "otherness" '. This is a recipe for the most extreme kind of alienation, disassociating art from nature on the one hand, and art and nature from the human subject on the other. More than

this: in denying, as it must, tradition, history and the poetic voice, it can only be a prescription for de-culturizing art; as Goossen himself says in the same article, 'the spectator is not given symbols but facts, to make of what he can. They do not direct his mind nor call up trusted cores of experience, but lead him to the point where he must evaluate his own response.' His use of the word 'response' is significant in this context, in that it situates the aesthetic experience almost exclusively in the psycho-physical as opposed to the socio-cultural domain. Nations, tribes and creeds are thus dissolved in favour of the disassociated individual and the purpose of American abstract art is revealed as the abstraction of culture itself. Herein lies its power as an instrument of American colonization.

Following the Venice Biennale of 1980, the most outspoken of the American critics spoke disparagingly of the new German and Italian painting, calling it 'nationalistic', 'regressive' and 'reactionary'. After the 1982 Documenta exhibition the most influential of New York's left-wing critics, Benjamin Buchloh, went as far as to suggest that their nationalism coupled with their 'expressionism' allied them to fascist forces to work in modern societies.[11] Perhaps such views are best understood as part of the New York art world's siege mentality at this time. After all, the Teutonic hordes are at the gate; some are already within the citadel. The Italian carnival is parading in their streets and even the British are beginning to throw off the yoke of 25 years of cultural domination.

NOTES

1 Quoted in Pierre Cabanne, 'The window into something else', *Dialogues with Marcel Duchamp*, Thames & Hudson, London, 1971.

2 WPA (Works Progress Administration) was funded by the state for the 'useful' employment of artists. It organized projects sited in factories, universities, schools and hospitals.

3 In an article entitled 'We can win the battle for the mind of Europe' and sub-headed, 'The Europeans, even those behind the iron curtain, can still be swung to Western culture', *New York Times* magazine, 25 April 1948.

4 Clement Greenberg, one-time member of the 'popular front', wrote for the magazines *Partisan Review*, *Nation* and *Horizon*. He was cited as a Trotsky sympathizer by a member of McCarthy's Committee for Un-American Activities.

5 In 1958 Sir William Coldstream, professor at the Slade School of Fine Art from 1949 to 1975, took charge of a policy committee charged with making recommendations for restructuring British art education. His committee reported in 1960. The task of implementing his recommendations was passed to a separate committee chaired by Sir John Summerson.

6 In a foreword to *Europe-America: The Different Avant-gardes*, Ricci, Milan, 1976, a catalogue to an exhibition of contemporary European and American art held in Milan. In this essay he plots the differences between European and American art.

7 Harold Rosenberg's most important works are *Tradition of the New*, University of Chicago Press, Chicago, 1959 and *Anxious Object*, University of Chicago Press, Chicago, 1964.

8 Born in France, Duchamp came to refer to America after the mid-forties as his 'adopted country' simply because he spent more time there than anywhere else.

9 Frederico Garcia Lorca (1899–1936) was executed by Franco's militia during the Spanish Civil War. The quotation is from an essay on the Spanish poet Góngora translated in part in Arturo Barea, *Lorca: The Poet and his People*, Cooper Square Publishers Inc., New York, 1973.

10 Goossen – the full title of this catalogue was *The Art of the Real*: 'Today's real makes no direct appeal to the emotions, nor does it involve any uplift but instead offers itself in the form of simple, irreducible, irrefutable object.'

11 In 'Documenta 7: A Dictionary of Received Ideas', *October*, No. 22, Fall 1982, pp. 105-26.

NEW
PAINTING
AND
OLD
PAINTING

A PRECARIOUS SPONTANEITY
OR AN OUTMODED TRADITION?

ALEXANDER MOFFAT

Towards the end of the seventies, with Modernism firmly stuck in the straight-jacket of its own orthodoxies and dogmas, everyone became bored with art about art. The experimental artist was no longer an embattled figure: the artist had come to terms with 'capitalist' society – indeed had become subservient to it. The tendency to present art history as a succession of avant-garde styles in a process of formal evolution began to be questioned by the many, instead of the few, and the idea of Modernism as a creative force taking up a position against the established order was finally seen to be hollow.

Today a great debate is going on about 'the end of Modernism' and what is to be done in the new 'Post-Modernist' phase. In this discussion the situation in painting has been crucial; in perhaps the most significant development of the past five years, we have witnessed a re-emergence of figurative imagery in painting. All that has been disallowed for twenty-five years – history, literature, story-telling – all of this has flooded back into painting with a terrible vengeance. And it has provoked more heated argument, more critical hostility, more emotional response than any new movement since Action painting in the late forties.

Put in simple terms, painting after 1945 has been regarded as a battle between Abstraction and Figuration. By the early sixties it seemed as if the hegemony of Abstraction was assured. The claims of the great European pioneers and their American followers that Abstraction would supersede all other forms of painting were avidly pursued in the decade following the end of the war, and a tradition of abstract painting, epitomized by Kandinsky and Mondrian and then Pollock and Kline, Newman and Rothko, became accepted as *the* twentieth-century tradition, the 'mainstream' of our times. The historicist view of modern art, then applied with gusto, condemned all figurative modes of painting as outdated and retrograde, and, to make matters worse, figurative painting became associated with the Stalinist left or with dull academic hacks. During the seventies, however, Abstract painting was forced to give way as the vanguard movement to a group of Conceptual artists for whom the idea or concept of art outweighed the finished product. The Conceptualists played down formalist and imagist objectives in favour of investigative exercises. By abandoning traditional forms of painting and sculpture they also replaced the art object – the finished

Frank Auerbach
PORTRAIT OF SANDRA
1974
Marlborough Fine Art
(London) Ltd

permanent art work – by a process, a strategy, relating to language, history and politics. Within this framework of ideas the difficulties in establishing any kind of painterly image as a serious alternative proved enormous.

In the sixties and seventies figurative painting developed in opposition to the established Modernist ethos so that attitudes and positions were developed in a hostile climate. A remarkable group of figurative painters came through those years with their reputations intact, and their presence, at the time, held out possibilities for those who hoped for a figurative renaissance. Francis Bacon, Lucian Freud, Frank Auerbach, Peter de Francia, David Hockney and R. B. Kitaj were the artists who constituted the 'School of London', a title invented by Kitaj. In 1976, Kitaj put together an exhibition centred on this group, entitled 'The Human Clay'. He made a claim for the renewal of a specific European tradition of pictorial description allied to a concern for the social value of a humanist art. 'Don't listen to the fools that say either that pictures of people can be of no consequence or that painting is finished. There is much to be done.'[1] Throughout the latter part of the seventies Kitaj became a leading polemicist for a return to the human figure as the great subject matter for art, but with his emphasis on the role of life-drawing he was accused of fighting a rearguard action on behalf of outmoded traditionalism.

It was also during the late seventies that the story of modern art began to be scrutinized and reassessed in the light of several important historical exhibitions which were mounted at the Centre Pompidou in Paris. These shows, 'Paris/Berlin' (1977), 'Paris/

Moscow' (1979) and 'Les Réalismes' (1981), along with 'Neue Sachlichkeit' (1978) at the Hayward Gallery and 'Beckmann's Triptychs' (1980) at the Whitechapel Gallery in London, made art and artists that had been ignored in the Modernist history books visible again. There was now a new context in which to view the art of the twentieth century.

Seizing eagerly on this, and inspired by Kitaj's example, the artist and critic Timothy Hyman selected a large exhibition called 'Narrative Paintings' which toured Britain in 1979-80. Concentrating on contemporary British painting, Hyman brought into focus many artists who were hitherto unknown – Ken Kiff, Peter Darach, Andrzej Jackowski – and placed them alongside Paolozzi, Hockney, Kitaj and Hodgkin. After an impressive attack on the suffocating taboos of Modernism, he expanded his ideas about a new heroic, visionary language of figuration and in his introduction quoted Léger: 'a return to "great subjects" . . . it seems to me is the normal logical direction for the contemporary evolution of easel painting, after the whole gamut of explorations that has been made since Impressionism'. He ended by saying that he would like 'Narrative Paintings' to be seen as a gesture of encouragement, 'to help hasten the thaw – the full flowering that's still probably a year or two hence.'[2] Little did Hyman realize that the figuration which would eventually flood the Western art world would be of an entirely different sort; a figuration nurtured in the avant-garde galleries of Germany and Italy and inspired by a type of nationalism unknown in Western European art for over half a century.

In Germany too, there was a group of painters who made a stand in the sixties and seventies against the cultural status quo. The work of Baselitz, Hödicke and Lüpertz became increasingly influ-

ential and they were joined by Kiefer, Penck and Immendorf as the leading painters of their generation. After Hitler's war, Germany had no modern art to speak of, and German artists apologetically turned to the international styles of first France and then America in order to pick up the pieces. As West Germany became politically and culturally more confident, its artists, writers, composers and filmmakers became conscious of the need to create an art which was not second-hand in origin. The difficult task of exploring the oppressive burden of their own recent cultural and political past began, as well as a rediscovery of German artistic models prior to the Nazi years. By the late sixties German art had a new sense of direction.

With figurative painting thought to be obsolete, and Expressionism considered a decadent style, the new German painting has proved a puzzling and complex issue to many. Clearly, there is a need for a new encounter with and an understanding of the Expressionist phenomenon. To do this we must go back to a debate which raged in German émigré circles in the thirties, and involved Georg Lukács, Ernst Bloch, Walter Benjamin, T.W. Adorno and many other exiles from Nazi Germany.[3] What was at stake involved the central dilemma of Expressionism. Was Expressionism the progressive and revolutionary movement it often claimed to be, or did it, in fact, nourish the rise of Nazism? The pacifism of the early Expressionists and their idealistic sense of mission were partly due to a wish to change humankind. Along with visions of universal brotherhood and a militant utopianism, they also embraced an

Georg Baselitz
DIE GROSSEN FREUNDE/THE GREAT FRIENDS
1965
Museum moderner Kunst Wien, Leihgabe
Sammlung Ludwig, Aachen

intense subjectivism and a return to primitivism. It is this aspect of Expressionism which is regarded by some as a regressive tendency, a deliberate lapse into barbarism. Others, on the contrary, saw it as regeneration in the face of decadence. In this context the connections between Expressionism and Teutonic racialism are of special importance, for despite fundamental differences, Nazism and Expressionism were not without common features. It is this historical problem which colours our views of contemporary German painting.

Georg Lukács found Expressionism a subjective and irrational mode of apprehending reality and, as a result, championed an art which appeared objective and realistic. Though many of Lukács's arguments were dismissed as apologies for 'socialist realism' (and at times they were just that), his criticism of Expressionism cannot be ignored. Ernst Bloch was also critical of irrational mystification, but he argued that Expressionism remained a radical indictment of the status quo in so far as it manifests a 'dream content', which becomes a central part of the revolutionary 'inheritance'. Expressionist experiments attempting the freeing of the unconscious and the fantastic abounded, and for Bloch this led to the possibility of seeing reality in new ways. Lukács overlooked the fact that Expressionism contained many elements, both progressive and reactionary, and that a truly revolutionary art is always an art of

diversity.

The new German painters also see Expressionism as an emancipatory force, freeing creativity and life from repressive social and cultural restraints. The seriousness of the best of the German painters cannot be doubted. Not only have they opened up a dialogue with their own cultural and political history and with the masters of German Expressionism, they have also assimilated a knowledge of post-war Abstract painting and of the theories and practices of Conceptual Art. Indeed, their work constitutes a kind of 'conceptual expressionism' and can be seen as a figurative painting that follows on from abstraction.

The involvement of the German painters in European political and artistic struggles and their experiences in a divided Berlin, in Düsseldorf and in the Eastern bloc may make their work appear nationalistic and removed from the intentions of British artists, but in dominating the international art world German painting has become a kind of backdrop against which all other painting must be assessed. The main critical debate over the return of painting and of the image, its role as a radical art form and its capacity to adopt a critical stance, centres on German painting, giving it a significance which extends beyond Germany's borders.

Although British painting has tended towards other influences, there are a number of important artists who have looked to a northern and more spiritual art rather than to the Mediterranean land-

John Bellany
BETHEL
1967
Southampton Art Gallery

scape of pleasure. The paintings of Bacon, Kossoff, Auerbach, Kiff and Bellany all reveal an awareness and practice of Expressionism. Bellany, in particular, derives his language of painting from Munch and Beckmann, and like Baselitz, his German contemporary, worked in an Abstract Expressionist style during his student years. He considers his Scottish cultural heritage as a treasure chest, as something of awesome emotional power, capable of sustaining and enriching his life's work. Exiled from his roots and living in London, his gestural handling of paint was admired, but his content quietly ignored until recently. Whereas in Germany, Baselitz's art and ideas became increasingly influential and useful, Bellany remained a strange outsider on the London scene, and only in the past few years has his work received proper critical attention. But Bellany, along with Kossoff, Auerbach, Bacon and Kiff, is genuinely Expressionist, and thus differs profoundly from the many artists who have jumped on to the Expressionist bandwagon.

Many of the distinguishing features of the New Painting were displayed to good advantage in a huge survey called 'Zeitgeist', shown in Berlin towards the end of 1982 and basically an orchestrated show of strength by the new German and Italian painters. The challenging and excessive nature of their images, full of contradictions and tensions, made a tremendous and potentially liberating impact on young artists, bringing about an overnight transformation in attitudes to making art. This exhibition, coupled with the success of the new European painters in the art markets of New York, turned figurative expressionism into international fashion. The extravagant promotion of the new painting via the Biennales, art fairs, galleries and museums has falsified real achievement, and the triumph of the Germans in particular has led to a raw, bombastic, daubing method of painting, overloaded with mythological emblems and faked primitive values, which is emulated all over the world. The reliance of many of the new painters on images which are recognizable as belonging to art, to art history, combined with their nostalgia and revivalism, has resulted in much that is little more than feeble pastiche. Whether their work is Expressionist or neo-Classical in flavour, many new young painters simply plunder from the past in a cynical and modish manner.

The social and cultural experience of the sixties and seventies, which witnessed a change from idealism and optimism to retrenchment and resignation, has affected the way in which the new generation of painters sees itself. Their aim to be simply artists of their own generation, their rejection of a hard-won mastery over materials and ideas, their emphasis on spontaneous and violent experience, have alienated the new painters from the older 'survivors', those painters who struggled against the Modernist tide for so long. (It is impossible to imagine, for instance, any of the successful younger painters travelling regularly to the National Gallery, as Auerbach has done for many years in order to study the procedures of Signorelli and to draw from a Rembrandt. Any excursion of this nature would be to look for suitable and instant quotations.) All too suddenly the survivors saw their dreams replaced with small ambition and crushing banality. They saw too the possibilities of a wide-ranging approach to the problems of figuration narrowed down once again, to a limited and one-dimensional stylistic solution.

Although the current focus on New Painting seems to have limited the development of figurative art, encouraging a largely negative and uncritical self-expression, the fact remains that painting per se is now worthy of serious discussion as a radical and contemporary art. Painting today is inevitably about what is possible in painting and its implications for the future. This controversy, this struggle to proclaim what is truly the authentic voice of painting, will continue in the foreground, and not in a cultural backwater as was the case in the sixties and seventies.

Britain has usually remained outside the main currents of European intellectual and artistic thought and this insularity has both its good and bad points. British painters have managed to avoid the worst excesses of the New Painting and as a result show up favourably when comparison is allowed — and this is possible more often as British art begins to travel and more European and American shows arrive here. The 'pluralism' of the past five years has also released a British eccentricity, exposing a pronounced individualism which contrasts positively with the slavish imitations pouring out of Europe and America.

Of course, the hopes and ideals that many had for painting have not materialized and perhaps never will. As the purist aesthetic and formal preciousness of the seventies dwindled away, the social relevance and unity so desired by Kitaj etc. during the past two decades have failed to emerge. On the one hand we have a modish, slick art encouraged by economic interests to assume a whirlwind tempo of change. On the other, we have a number of artists attempting the difficult task of establishing a relationship to the past, without the self-conscious homage that affected so many former attempts. Certainly artists must engage with and build from the present melting pot of conflicting ideas if there is to be a new sense of purpose and authority in the art of the next two decades. Modernism in its utopian period was motivated by a concept of the future, but has not proved to be the triumph of progress once proclaimed. The moral and spiritual quest of the modern pioneers to shape a new language for twentieth-century art was replaced by the cult of novelty which ended up with an acceptable product, capable of instant consumption by those very forces Modernism had set out to oppose. But after Modernism, what next? Is the current preoccupation with the past a symptom of a reactionary, anti-Modernist conservatism? Or is it, on the other hand, a genuine attempt to forge a deeper, more meaningful and humane relationship between artist and public? Those questions will be posed for many years to come, just as the central problems of the past hundred years have remained unsolved – art as uncompromising formal innovation or a language of accessibility? As a luxury product or as an ideological/political tool? There are some who believe that solutions are imperative, but posterity, with a fairer sense of perspective, may not wish to judge such complex issues.

NOTES

1 *The Human Clay*, catalogue to an exhibition selected by R. B. Kitaj; Arts Council of Great Britain, 1976.

2 *Narrative Paintings*, catalogue to an exhibition selected by Timothy Hyman; Arnolfini, Bristol, 1979.

3 The debate about Expressionism ran from 1934 through to 1938 and was conducted mainly in the pages of two Moscow émigré journals edited by Johannes Becher, *Internationale Literatur* and *Das Wort*. *Aesthetics and Politics* (New Left Books, London, 1977) publishes key texts from this controversial debate. Those taking part included: Theodor Wiesengrund Adorno (1903–69), German philosopher, composer and Kultur-Kritik, who was a pupil of Alban Berg in Vienna and a member of Schoenberg's circle in Berlin. He emigrated to the USA in 1934, returning to Germany after the war and taught at Frankfurt University. Ernst Bloch (1885–1977) was one of the most idiosyncratic Marxist philosophers of his time. After emigrating to the USA in 1933 he returned to East Germany in 1948, where he was made professor of philosophy at Leipzig. In 1961 he moved to West Germany. In his two great works, *Vom Geist der Utopie* and *Das Prinzip Hoffnung*, he attempts to reconstruct a 'philosophy of hope' on the basis of Marxism and Jewish utopianism. Walter Benjamin (1892–1940), German essayist and literary critic, emigrated to Paris after Hitler came to power. His major works include essays on Baudelaire, Proust and Kafka. He committed suicide while fleeing to Spain to escape from the Nazis. Georg Lukács (1885–1971), Hungarian philosopher and literary critic, lived in Berlin from 1919 until 1933. Emigrating to the Soviet Union after the Nazis took over, he returned to Budapest in 1945. His major works of criticism include essays on nineteenth-century realism, the historical novel and Thomas Mann, as well as on Marx, Hegel and Nietzsche.

MINISTERS
OF
MISRULE

MARJORIE ALLTHORPE-GUYTON

British art is probably less insular than it has ever been. Everywhere, but especially among young artists, you will find an interested view of current German and Italian art. British artists want to be informed, yet at the same time there is a resistance to discipleship. Although luminaries like Joseph Beuys are acknowledged, there is currently a suspicion of gurus. The idea of schools no longer obtains as it did, say, in the sixties. For instance, on the basis of art world talk and media coverage one would expect New Expressionism, or New Image painting, to be widespread, but this is not the case; the new idiom has been acknowledged but certainly not seen as a panacea. British artists have been unwilling, or too detached, to involve themselves in *angst* on a German scale.

Nonetheless, British artists in the eighties are likely to have visited Documentas and Biennales and to have gone, for example, to the major Beckmann exhibition in Berlin in 1984. Nor is the idea of going to live abroad such a great shock to the psyche as it might once have been. For any younger artist there is a wealth of potential directions which might be followed, even the temptation to think that anything goes, and this can be as disabling or constraining as any modernist straightjacket might have been to the previous generation. In addition it is as clear now as it ever has been in the past that there is a strong market demand for novelty or readily identifiable originality. This art, to be seen largely in dealers' shows and in vanguard galleries, can be difficult to keep track of in any sense you care to mention. Can it, for example, be understood in terms of a British tradition, or is such a tradition entirely beside the point in relation to today's art?

If these questions are to be argued it ought to be with reference to material in the show, material which ranges right the way from traditional painting and sculpture through to video, film and performance. For instance, one of the most intriguing items here is Sandra Goldbacher's *Polka Dots and Moonbeams*, a video of 1983. Ostensibly this is a feminist work which makes use of promotion video idioms and up-to-the-minute scratch techniques. It concentrates on a gallery of girls, their beauty offset by a shaven-headed punk from Derek Jarman's film *Jubilee*. In the foreground a Gorgon of sorts dominates an androgynous youth. It takes for its subjects male/female identity, narcissism, fetishism, voyeurism. The film's implication is that attitudes which feminists have deplored in men are also indulged by women. In other words sexual identities are challenged by an artist whose ideas have moved beyond feminist positions of the seventies. Whatever shades of meaning might be identified in *Polka Dots and Moonbeams* its form is almost that of a commercial promo-video, with the difference that it markets an idea rather than a product. Unavoidably it raises questions about the importance of the promo-video as one of *the* contemporary forms, just as it points to feminism as one of the dynamic ideologies of the eighties. In other words if we are to come to terms with a work such as this it has to be through politics, psychoanalysis and commerce; talk of traditional art will do us no good, at the outset at least.

Similar elements appear in Jayne Parker's black-and-white film, *I Dish*, which has castration anxiety as one of its subjects. A young man obsessively washes his genitals and recounts, it seems, the story of a recent trauma. The woman listens silently; we see close-ups of her eyes and mouth. She meticulously skins, guts, bones and cooks a fish. The film disturbs commonplace psychoanalytical notions of male and female identity. *She* appears as fetishist and voyeur; the male becomes the object of her gaze. Parker, like Goldbacher, is inverting and even subverting some current dogmas in psychoanalytical and feminist thought. Not only does *I Dish* suggest that there are no readymade and reliable answers, but it challenges the very idea of such answers, and in its turn asserts the priority of imagination, of art.

If a list of the major issues of the day was to be drawn up it would necessarily include the status of women, racial prejudice, unemployment, industrial dereliction, nuclear politics. None of these are matters to be taken lightly, and in public debate none *are* taken lightly, but artists don't play to these rules. Neither Parker nor Goldbacher debates the issues in the style of journalists or researchers; rather they re-form those issues as imaginative constructs. The argument remains identifiable, thrown into even sharper relief, but at the same time it has been liberated, and shown to be more than a pragmatic matter.

John Hyatt, too, explores areas of concern current in post-industrial Britain. Patriotism takes the stage; under a red, white and blue sky a lion and a unicorn balance precariously at the deep end of a

Hockneyesque swimming pool. Hyatt violates that Californian Shangri-La, but enough of it lingers to break the northern darkness. Texts unfurl like banners, pylons go on the warpath, men ride pigs, the circus comes to town. Art confronts the factory and labour, and that harsh world in its turn is leavened by the carnival of art.

But surely none of this is alien to British tradition? Most obviously Hyatt continues in the line of Hogarth when he satirizes self-importance in artists (the 'pile-on' painters as he calls them). Like Hogarth he also energizes what he satirizes, and the result is as much carnival as social document. More recent parallels appear in the art of Edward Burra and of Stanley Spencer. In Burra's cafés and dockside dives the tawdry is transformed into a kind of lurid folk cabaret. In Spencer's Cookham gardens English matrons romp like players in a Breughel burlesque. Both artists negotiate between opposites, between pantomime and social deprivation in one case and between wanton revelry and respectability in the other. Francis Bacon, too, has almost always invoked oppositions. He suggests the sublime or the grotesque or the terminal through anatomical fragmentation and references to tragic and heroic lives, those of Van Gogh and of Aeschylus's Greeks. Bacon touches on alienation, isolation and, more particularly, on the simultaneity of good and evil. This fundamental ambiguity underlies the aggressive yet seductive work of Gilbert & George, where a powerful sense of evil can permeate images of extreme beauty. As they put it, their works 'have a modern, inverted symbolism of life. A kind of subversive form.'[1]

Described in this way none of these artists

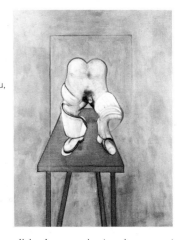

Francis Bacon
STUDY OF THE
HUMAN BODY
1982
Musée National
d'Art Moderne,
Centre Georges Pompidou,
Paris

appears to be responsible, in any electoral sense at least. Low life has become a cabaret in Burra's lurid tableaux. Bacon's casualties are often as beautiful as they are tragic. Goldbacher and Hyatt are both as entertaining as they are didactic. Yet none of them could be described as inconsequential or trivializing for they all consider some of the most troubling preoccupations of their times. The process combines extreme irreverence with high seriousness, and verges on the convulsive. In art of this sort preconceived categories are dissolved and fused to reappear in fantastic new forms. It is an art which is more exuberant than deliberative, and one which answers to our need for the solace of the fantastic without denying social and physical reality.

The fantastic: this is a term which can hardly be avoided in any discussion of contemporary culture. Naturalism is out of fashion. The trend was set in popular film in the late seventies, by *Star Wars*, an extraordinary pot-pourri of Walt Disney and Hollywood fairy tales and legends, and evolved to include Gothic horror, violence and sado-masochism, as exemplified by *Alien* and *The Evil Dead*. Advertising began to appropriate surrealist fantasy, and Magritte was invoked to underpin up-market smoking habits. In D. M. Thomas's novel *The White Hotel*, one of the publishing successes of the early eighties, a Freudian case history of female hysteria is re-narrated polyphonically, and unities of time, space and character are broken down. Thomas, drawing on several documentary sources, conflates hallucination and memory. He implies a symbiotic relationship between actual and fantasized experience; his characters can never be free from fantasy. As these idioms have become more familiar so they

Edward Burra
CAFE
1930
Southampton
Art Gallery

have become subject to more and more complex expression, as in Paul Cox's film of 1983, *Man of Flowers*, an elaborate fiction of the psyche.

The imagination and its constructions have rarely been of such interest. In scholarly terms this has meant new critical studies of the Gothic novel, of the fictions of Dostoevsky and Kafka.[2] In art it has meant a reawakened interest in Pre-Raphaelitism and in the painting of such symbolists as Gustave Moreau and Arnold Böcklin. It also means that art which might once have been dismissed as eccentric and thus marginalized can now be comprehended and given a critical context. But the real and underlying question here has less to do with increased critical sophistication than with the centrality of fantasy to these times.

Is this fantastic strain any more than an expression of theatricality and self-indulgence? Does it answer to anything deeper in our culture or in ourselves? One of the more challenging exhibits here is Stuart Brisley's display of plaster-filled and painted gloves from *The Georgiana Collection*, begun as a series in 1981. At one level it makes a clearly comprehensible social point: the discarded gloves can be seen as standing for waste in an indifferent culture. Their being caged complicates the meaning: it introduces an idea of containing or screening off society's surplus, both material and human. Of the inmates of a doss house, he wrote, in a Lewis Johnstone Gallery broadsheet of 1983, 'they refuse everything, and are slowly wilting. You can see that they have become representatives of another species, that species over there from the other side.' He suggests, both in this text and in much of his art, the idea of entropy, of a running down to a zero point where man, animal and object collapse, one into the other. At this zero point there exists something more like a torment of matter or primal flux and an absence of social and ethical values. All this is to say that on the one hand Brisley involves himself in society's problems, and that on the other he evokes an original state which precedes or underlies the social.

This 'original state' appears in the art on show here. It can be most obviously identified in the primal disturbance of Leon Kossoff's painted surfaces from which physical configurations begin to declare themselves. Something similar, but much more explicit, happens in Bill Woodrow's tableaux as banal, wasted material returns to vigorous life.

Decay, destruction, entropy: such terms recur because all these artists evoke ideas of an original raw state, not merely as something which might be worked on but as something of value in its own right, something inescapable, something not to be denied. A similar original state is to be seen in the painting of Paula Rego and Ken Kiff, where roughly hewn imagery and primary colours are insisted on. In Kiff's *The Feminine as Generous, Frightening and Serene* blood and paint are elided in an intricate metaphor. As in all Kiff's painting there is a powerful sense of life at a moment of emergence.

None of this can be thought of for long without psychoanalytical questions coming to mind. Freud identified a fundamental human desire for fusion, and Lacan in his turn referred to it as 'an eternal desire for the non-relationship of zero, where identity is meaningless'.[3] An ultimate symbol of this state of fusion is the sea. The sea, fluid and undefined, represents the unobtainable in Romantic art. Such a sea pervades Thérèse Oulton's large canvases where space and objects dissolve into each other. She gives form to what Byron called 'a sort of grey giddiness first, then nothingness'. Not that this fusion is always achieved; in Stephen Campbell's paintings nature is everywhere and in a constant state of metamorphosis, while man, exemplified by a lumbering tyro, appears perpetually unassimilable. Campbell's Gothic topography of enclosures, vaults and dark places raises the threat of separation and isolation.

Described thus the paintings of Oulton and Campbell take on existentialist qualities, but the art of that era focused on individual isolation, as something which might be palpably experienced. By contrast, the art of today is more discursive. Giacometti's figures, for example, inhabit real space, whereas Oulton's voids are hinted at and symbolized by bridges, stairways and walls, by details which might be read and calculated. Again at first sight John Murphy's painting *The Skeleton at the Feast. . . A Spectre is Haunting Europe* might be read existentially, as bearing on a human predicament. But it is far more cypher than substance, for it is incomplete, a ghost of itself, weighted down by a title drawn from the opening of Marx's *Communist Manifesto* of 1848. We are faced not with an image of physical remains but with an accusatory spectral presence, a tracing on the wall which is also a reminder of retribution. Murphy refers to Marx and brings to mind other Gothic hauntings, such as that of Maturin's Melmoth cursed by his own spectre.[4] Murphy's is also a literary kind of art in which extremes are mediated by intellect. In *The Skeleton* he refers obliquely to final things, to death and to revolution, through a messenger faint almost to the point of invisibility. Gilbert & George in their equally radical communications picture themselves as insubstantial, almost in a detached holographic form. They propose a lack of physical substantiality in themselves, and even in the world on which they report. They suggest instead the priority of images, and do so the more where extremes are involved. In this respect their work is comparable to that of the American painter and film-maker Jack Goldstein who exploits the beauty and unreality of war's pyrotechnics in immaculately air-brushed paintings that are as distanced and neutralized as the images they appropriate. In re-presenting these images, many of them from British war archives, Goldstein, like Michael Sandle, underlines the ambiguity of our response to technology and war, and shows how we may come to *desire* the objects of our repression and domination.

It is easy enough to describe this memory- and media-haunted art as post-modern and to leave it at that. Certainly it eschews absolutes and essentials, and pays little heed to the objective world. In line with the psychoanalysts it supposes reality to be an unstable construct of the imagination, subject to oceanic and other yearnings. But the imagination's capacity for invention prompts a counter-tendency towards the hieratic, towards an art which attempts a resolution of opposites. In John Davies's sculpted ensembles of the late seventies, clustered figures suggest events, interactions, interiority, a before and an after. Gradually these mysterious, yet tantalizingly interpretable groupings have been put aside, and the more recent heads, especially those on a giant scale, express, in an Assyrian or an Egyptian sense, nothing but themselves. Leonard McComb, never much of a fantasist, gives even more implacable expression to the hieratic in symmetrically posed standing figures. In McComb's case there is no question of radical change, of a turning away from an earlier style, but it is surely no accident that his imposing art with its sculptural qualities has only now been fully acknowledged, for it stands as a reproach and a challenge to contemporary enthusiasms. Yet at the same time McComb

Jack Goldstein
Untitled
1983
Lisson Gallery,
London

too is preoccupied by the difficulties of finding a form for what is beyond measure. During the period of his involvement with heroic portraiture he has worked on the coast of Anglesey on sea pieces in which the sea's immensity is conveyed fragmentarily. Tendencies towards the hieratic and intact provoke, it seems, the need to pursue the measureless or transcendental – and maybe this applies both individually and collectively. This simultaneity of opposites was also characteristic of Romantic art, of the watercolour art of J. S. Cotman for example, with its conjunction of fluid, natural forms and underlying order.

These contradictions are nowhere clearer than in the art of Stephen McKenna, represented here by the ruins of *Selinunte* and the fragments of *O, Ilium!* McKenna has an encyclopedic range of reference; in *O, Ilium!*, for example, twenty or so representations of sculpted figures hint both at myths and at their subsequent history in western painting, especially in the art of Poussin and David. In this well-stocked diorama ancient history stands as something to be read; it also ceases to be ancient history, for its fragments often look revivified to the point of ripeness. The ruins of *Selinunte* also look less than timeless; not only are they tumbled but they appear to have suffered a change of state, to have become organic. They carry about them a bloom of decay and this implication of the organic is expanded by the blood-red ground against which they lie. McKenna's work bears comparison with that of the Scottish sculptor Gareth Fisher in which there is as strong an emphasis on ripeness of surface. But McKenna's is also a complex dialectical art marked by a simultaneous interest in the hieratic and the discursive. At the same time as he was working on his tableau of ruin and ancient history he was making hieratic pictures of trees, quite as hermetic as any of Davies's heads or McComb's nudes.

Many qualities of contemporary art are embodied in McKenna's work. Like his contemporaries he moves between extremes of social and cultural discursiveness and the hieratic. Inherent in such a movement is the idea that the contemporary world invites both involvement and disengagement, both attracts and repels. This is a governing principle which accounts for the range of work in this exhibition quite as much as it accounts for tensions and ambiguities within individual pieces.

NOTES

1 'The believing world of Gilbert & George', conversation with Lynn MacRitchie, *Performance Magazine*, No. 29 (April/May 1984), p. 20.

2 Rosemary Jackson, *Fantasy, the Literature of Subversion*, Methuen, London, 1981. Rosemary Jackson extends the seminal study of Tzvetan Todorov, *The Fantastic: A Structural Approach to a Literary Genre*, translated by Richard Howard, Cornell University Press, New York, 1973.

3 Jacques Lacan, *The Language of the Self: The Function of Language in Psychoanalysis*, Johns Hopkins University Press, Baltimore, 1968, p. 191; Jackson, op. cit., p. 77.

4 Charles Robert Maturin, *Melmoth the Wanderer*, A. Constable & Co., Edinburgh, 1820, quoted by Jackson, op. cit., p. 105. Maturin's novel is usually regarded as the culmination of the English Gothic novel.

1
REINVENTING THE REAL WORLD

What I'm not hoping to do is to paint another picture because there are enough pictures in the world. I'm hoping to make a new thing for the world that remains in the mind like a new species of living thing. (Frank Auerbach)[1]

Unlike America, where the easel picture was more or less abandoned, painting in Britain in the seventies retained a viable position thanks to the integrity and practice of a number of artists, both abstract and figurative. John Hoyland and Gillian Ayres on the one hand, and Frank Auerbach and Leon Kossoff on the other, all represent a refusal to relinquish hard-won traditions in the face of fashion. Untouched by the need to reject the immediate past, these artists have shown that many possibilities still remain open to painting. In 1980, after a decade of hostility to painting, John Hoyland passionately argued that what painters such as these had in common was 'their "belief" in the medium of painting, in its directness, its responsiveness, both illusive and allusive, infinitely variable in behaviour, and alchemic in its magical fusions'. He went on to affirm, 'Painting doesn't need any gadgetry and disallows gimmickry. It survives unaided as a pure force.'[2] This belief permeates the work of all the artists represented here. Their assertion that the creative act is a struggle between the artist and the realization of the work of art, their commitment to the effectiveness of the painted mark and their desire to add to the ideas of painting form a vital and ambitious artistic programme which has proved capable of sustaining some of the most positive and remarkable painting now before the public. Above all they have demonstrated in their work, which in some cases spans a period from the mid-fifties to the present day, an unwavering sense of responsibility to the artistic traditions, both old and new, from which they sprang, and from which they have confronted the small ambitions of many contemporary 'manifestations' with paintings of vision and grandeur.

The view that painting has a past but not a future irritated many significant artists in the seventies who firmly believed in a language of expressive or depictive figuration, no matter how unmodern this was at the time. That the past lives on as a meaningful and inspirational source to artists like R. B. Kitaj, Frank Auerbach and Leonard McComb, is particularly evident from their work. These artists maintain that an unbroken tradition exists within the history of European art and have placed their relationship to it at the very heart of their practice. This involvement with a figurative language, long thought to have been rendered obsolete by the Cubist revolution earlier this century, has become a polemical issue of great importance.

The reclaiming of tradition presents figurative artists with problems which are largely connected to the breakdown, at the end of the last century, of the representational language of painting which had existed since the Renaissance. In the nineteenth century this language was questioned and opposed from within, gradually resulting in its destruction at the hands of the Impressionists, and of Gauguin and Cézanne. In the intervening period Modernism has left a legacy of alternative 'traditions' making it extremely difficult, both theoretically and practically, to reintegrate with this 'overthrown' tradition. Kitaj is among those who think otherwise, believing quite simply, that the innovations of the late nineteenth and early twentieth centuries have been misapplied in the subsequent search to produce an art which was exclusively 'new'. Instead he traces a continuous tradition from Giotto to Matisse, discovering a sense of continuity with and through the art of the great masters, which provides an active context for his own work and is more than just a valedictory homage.

Although many artists who have withdrawn from Modernist positions to return to an art of representation via a veneration for the past, have done so from reactionary motives, it does not mean that all returns to representational methods of painting are doomed to failure. The French masters Braque and Matisse did not renounce representation; Léger returned to the figure and Bonnard declined to take the Impressionist path to Abstraction. With Picasso, the representation of the human figure remained the creative core of his life's work. It would be foolish simply to dismiss a respect for tradition as reactionary and wrong, just as it would be equally foolish to imagine that an artist like Kitaj is an implacable opponent of the modern movement. His criticism of Modernism is centred on those ideologies which deny the depiction of the human figure, and he has argued that 'Modernism is dear to me. Fascism and Modernism are enemies. Fascism is *my* enemy. On that principle, Modernism is my friend. It cannot be otherwise. . . . There *are*, however, some reforms, some reformations, even some revolutions which will enrich our artistic lives from time to time.'[3] Kitaj's idea of reform is to give the human figure a central role in modern painting. His engagement with Modernism and his involvement in a painting of ideas set him far apart from the kind of figurative art which has continued to flourish in the academies. This dull traditionalism, made in opposition to all the glorious discoveries of modern art, is nothing more than a vaguely formulated parochialism, lacking in imagination and without the ability to reinterpret the world in any critical context.

Auerbach, Kossoff and McComb all put the past to use. There is no doubt that to them the paintings of old masters such as Rembrandt, Titian, Poussin and Chardin are not museum pieces, to be either copied by diligent art students or confined to the historical studies department. Auerbach's attachment to Rembrandt has nothing whatsoever to do with academic investigation. On the contrary, the paintings of Rembrandt are to Auerbach a living reality, speaking not only of history, but conveying a message which can inspire and transform life and art now. The long-term study of painting prior to the twentieth century is crucial to the procedures of Auerbach, Kossoff and McComb. Theirs is an art born of a prolonged struggle with the basic materials and methods of drawing and painting. There are no shortcuts, no superficial gestures, no contrived situations in their work. This rejection of the artificial has led to a love of things permanent, things substantial, and their close involvement with the subject brings an extraordinary intensity to their reinvention of the physical world. A devotion to the human figure takes many forms – Auerbach's glowing nudes, Kossoff's perceptive family groups, McComb's visionary portraits. They all derive from personal experience, but radiate an energy which far transcends the ordinary. Their achievement has been to balance reality and imagination in the direct observation of the motif, releasing on to paper and canvas a life-enhancing presence in grand and splendid images.

Howard Hodgkin's paintings are also about the presence of people, of friends, of intimate places and encounters. The special qualities of Hodgkin's work, which distinguish him as one of the most individual voices of British painting, have to do with the elusive nature of his depiction of nearness and distance. His pictures, with their well-ordered structures, are reticent and contemplative. Their luxurious qualities suggest a fusion of East and West (Hodgkin is a widely acknowledged expert on Indian painting), as well as an almost perfect harmony between feeling and form. His approach to the human figure is unique. 'I think if you want to make pictures of human beings now, you have to forget about the National Gallery and forget about photography. What you do next, I've no idea, there are no models. You've got to do it yourself.'[4]

Although Hodgkin is a figurative artist in every sense, his sensuous colour formulations, use of architectural framing devices and love of decorative pattern point to affinities with certain modes of Abstraction. He is greatly admired by Gillian Ayres and by John Hoyland who, in his selection of artists for the 1980 Hayward Annual, attempted to break down artificial distinctions between abstraction and figuration. In an introductory section to what was essentially a survey of Abstract painting, Hoyland placed a variety of artists, including Hodgkin, Auerbach, Caulfield and Caro, who had all in his estimation set standards for British art in the sixties and seventies. In the catalogue he explained his personal choice of artists and view of painting: 'Some are very abstract while others contain strong figurative associations . . . None see their art or the conventions they use as exclusive; many of those working figuratively are fervent admirers of abstract art and vice versa. Indeed, many of the abstract painters were excellent figurative artists at one time. The path for all of them is not an easy one.'[5]

The decline of mainstream Abstraction over the past twenty years, although less pronounced in this country than in Europe, led here to its slow retreat from view. From the prominent position held by the St Ives painters in the late fifties, when Patrick Heron, Peter Lanyon and Roger Hilton began to establish considerable reputations, and after the impact of the first wave of American Abstract Expressionism on British painting, by the 1970s this tradition of painting only really survived as a minority concern in the pages of *Artscribe* and in the studios at the Stockwell Depot in South London. Tim Hilton described the scene there: 'In this dismal setting, for years, when the painting tradition seemed to most to be underground, a kind of abstract art was made that had quite large scale, softly broken paint, any amount of texture, not a lot of pronounced drawing, no dominant image, and harmonious rather than contrasting colour. This was in fact the international style of the time. It had its counterpart in New York, not so much because the British were following the Americans as because painters on both sides of the Atlantic had, by now, a common inheritance. The difference was that in England the work was made at the nadir of painting's public fortunes.'[6] The tradition of the new had overtaken Abstract painting. Abstraction itself now had a history and had, in many cases, become confined to the working out of a narrow idiom, restricted by what had also become academic traditions.

Are certain traditions and styles incapable of conveying ideas in a fresh and vigorous way, or does the validity of a style depend on particular historical circumstances? How and when does a style wear itself out, thus losing its power of meaningful utterance? Clement Greenberg, in addressing this problem, thought that it was 'a question of time and quality, how many people do it'. His explanation of the rise and fall of Abstract Expressionism was that 'having produced an art of major importance, it turned into a school, then into a manner, and finally into a set of mannerisms. Its leaders attracted imitators, many of them, and then some of these leaders took to imitating themselves.'[7] For too long, Abstract painting lived in the reflected glory of that optimistic period in the fifties when the cause of Abstraction was regarded as a heroic struggle in the defence of art and culture against a philistine onslaught of reactionary forces. That generation of American artists carried on the idealist traditions of high culture as a separate activity from both social and political reality, by their identification with the artist's unlimited freedom of expression and their stance as the spokesmen of the enlightened. The eventual reaction, which took place in the sixties – to an art of amusement and popular appeal – placed

Abstract painting under pressure and, to a new generation of artists, Abstraction appeared to be a defunct movement, concerned only with formal and aesthetic problems of its own making. For those reasons, recent Abstract painting has tended to be ignored and under-valued. Despite this state of affairs, Gillian Ayres, Basil Beattie and John Hoyland have produced an impressive body of work over the past five years. Remarkable for its sustained innovation and the quality of its ideas, their work is a tribute to the modern spirit at its most courageous. All these artists share a vision of painting which affirms and which celebrates, in vibrant and resplendent colours, life and nature. The bold and expressive paintings which have flowed from Gillian Ayres's studio in Wales in the past few years are imbued with a love of painting and pigment, reminding one of her statement that 'Titian, Rubens, and Matisse are the greatest painters, unashamedly, of sheer beauty – but they also use the medium to the fullest in every sense before or since, plus a complete combination of heart and minds.'[8] This sensuality, this richness of paint and colour, are also characteristic of the paintings of Beattie and Hoyland. In their latest works shapes or islands of colour have become heavier presences, giving their paintings a more structured, composed sense of unity and avoiding the pitfalls of a meandering improvisation. That they have also avoided the tendency to 'go into production', a fault which characterizes so much successful art of the post-war years, is yet another tribute to their flourishing creative powers.

The importance of the work of all the artists in this section is now beginning to be properly recognized. It is significant that this has emerged after much trial and error through a relationship with painting which stretches, in all cases, over a career of thirty years or more. The understanding of what it takes to make great art, the idea that quality comes from a lifetime of devotion to craft and the acquiring of skills, has given their work an authority that speaks powerfully for itself. David Bomberg wrote many years ago, 'An artist whose integrity sustains his strength to make no compromise with expediency is never degraded'.[9] The artists represented here more than testify to the authenticity of Bomberg's statement. They have shown by their resolute activity that if art is to survive as a major force, it must address larger issues than a dialogue with itself; it must retain its claim to seriousness over and above any kind of superficial enterprise, reinvesting in a greater sense of purpose and advancing towards a deeper spirituality, if it is to truly release a meaningful creativity into the world.

ALEXANDER MOFFAT

NOTES

1 Interview with Catherine Lampert, published in *Frank Auerbach*, catalogue to an Arts Council of Great Britain exhibition, 1978.

2 In the introduction to *Hayward Annual*, catalogue to Arts Council of Great Britain exhibition, 1980.

3 Interview with Timothy Hyman, 'A return to London', *London Magazine*, February 1980.

4 Interview with Timothy Hyman, *Artscribe*, No. 15, December 1978.

5 In the introduction to *Hayward Annual*, catalogue to Arts Council of Great Britain exhibition, 1980.

6 Tim Hilton, 'A force against the Basilisk', *Hayward Annual*, catalogue to Arts Council of Great Britain exhibition, 1980.

7 Interview with James Faure Walker, *Artscribe*, No. 10, January 1978.

8 *Notes on Paintings*, catalogue to touring exhibition, Museum of Modern Art, Oxford, 1981.

9 *David Bomberg: The Later Years*, catalogue to exhibition at Whitechapel Art Gallery, London, 1979.

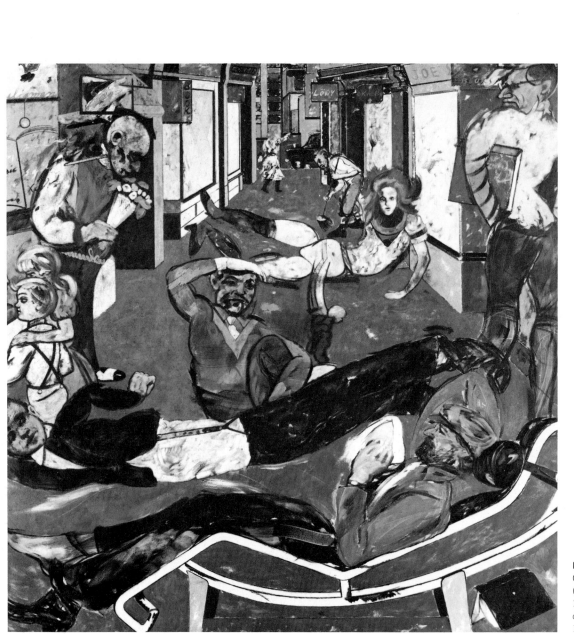

R. B. KITAJ
CECIL COURT, LONDON WC2
(THE REFUGEES)
1983-4
oil on canvas
182.9 x 182.9 cm

FRANK AUERBACH
EUSTON STEPS – STUDY
1980-1
oil on board
122 x 152.4 cm

LEON KOSSOFF
FIDELMA IN A RED CHAIR
1982
oil on board
62.2 x 48.2 cm

GILLIAN AYRES
A BELT OF STRAW AND IVY BUDS
1983
oil on canvas
310 x 167.6 cm

HOWARD HODGKIN
SOUVENIR
1981
original screenprint on
arches aquarelle mould-
made paper
114.3 x 139.7 cm

LEONARD McCOMB
ROCK AND SEA, ANGLESEY
1983
pencil, watercolour and
ink on handmade paper
457.5 x 457.5 cm

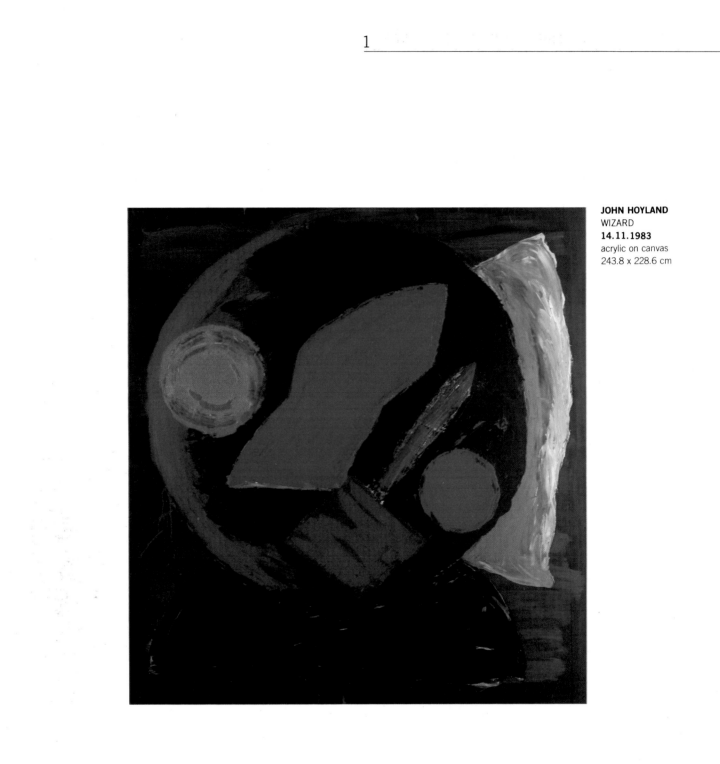

JOHN HOYLAND
WIZARD
14.11.1983
acrylic on canvas
243.8 x 228.6 cm

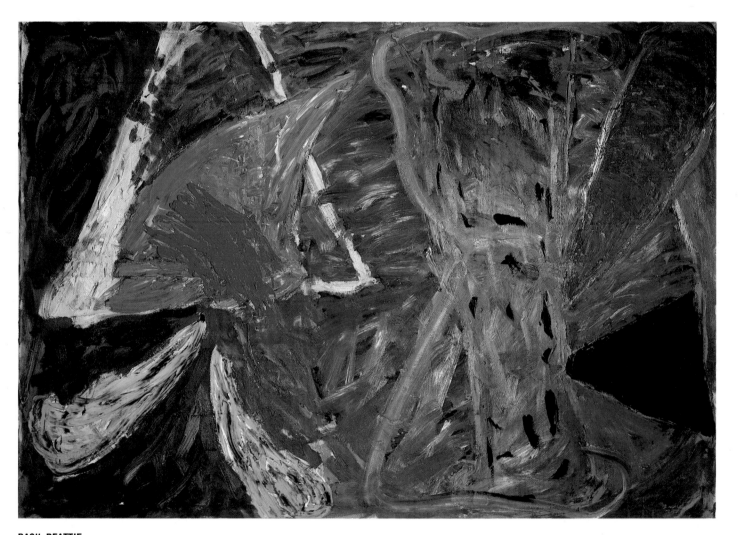

BASIL BEATTIE
NORTH MARCH
1984
acrylic and oil on cotton duck
213 x 306 cm

2
ORIGINS

For if we knew what original man was, we could declare what today's man is not.
(Barnett Newman)[1]

In 1982, 531,000 people visited Stonehenge. Few would agree with the testy view of Dr Johnson: 'to go and see one druidical temple is only to see that there is nothing for there is neither art nor power in it, and seeing one is quite enough'! Few would argue that there is not a persistent survival of custom and ritual in Western popular culture which has provided a tenuous link with our 'primitive' origins. Since Rousseau, modern man has thought himself to be cut off 'from his original (often historically primitive) nature and . . . from his essential (inherent and permanent) nature'.[2] This alienation has been a continual concern of the artist, especially since the Romantic period. It has manifested itself in a recurrent interest in past cultures. Artists have sought to express the spiritual and the sensual in the human imagination — the divine in man — much in the sense that the visionary poet–artist, Blake, gave to his poignant engraving in *The Gates of Paradise* of a man climbing a ladder to the moon: 'What is Man! I found him beneath a Tree. Water. Earth. Air. Fire. At length for Hatching ripe he breaks the shell. Alas! My Son! My Son! I want! I want!' This reaching for the infinite and for primal energy, sexual and imaginative, has consistently resurfaced, phoenix-like, in contemporary art. It has coexisted alongside more formal concerns; it broke with force in American painting of the forties, in the painting of Pollock, Rothko, Barnett Newman and Clyfford Still. Aspects of primitivism pervade the work of several artists in other sections of the show and in the following group of artists we see what Wilhelm Worringer described as a primal instinct in primitive man, a feeling for the 'thing in itself'.[3]

At the core of Anish Kapoor's strange and seductive forms is a contradiction between attraction and repulsion. They draw their power and presence from ambiguities, from the dualism of male and female, material and spiritual, fecund and destructive, geometric and organic. The present work developed after a visit to India in 1979; the first pieces were closely related to external forms of Indian architecture — the ziggurat and dome. Later they take on more fleshly shape, as functionaries of myth, like Kali with 'skin like the petal of a blue lotus at night'. But though savagely sexual, the things themselves are hard and *unsensual*, made of ground chalk and plaster, covered and circled by powdered pigment. They are what Kandinsky called 'the fantastic in hardest matter'. They forbid touch. The new pieces are made of even less yielding stuff: wood, fibreglass and resin covered in cement and mud painted a solid colour and skimmed with powder. They are like berries too poisonous to eat.

Richard Deacon's sculptures, on the other hand, are reassuringly real, clearly articulated from familiar materials: linoleum, laminated wood, cloth, galvanized and sheet steel. Their making is unconcealed: the joins, the rivets and screws are more than obvious. But their true identity eludes us, it is poised between perception and experience; the image — a sort of shoe, a hat, a head, an eye, a mouth, an ear, a musical instrument — is a new *thing* created from that tension.

Rilke, the Austrian poet, called this, the redeeming power of art to translate outer experience into a new reality of feeling, *Weltinnenraum* or world inner space. In Rilke, Richard Deacon finds an imagery whose concreteness is a quality of Deacon's own work. For the poet, Song is being. For the artist, it is the Object. Like sonata form, the drawing imposes a clarity, a control on Deacon's work which contains the conflict between subjective passion and order. The line binds opposites: the inner and outer, the skeleton and the skin, the male and the female. Blake thought it was Life itself:

> . . . Circumscribing & Circumcising the excrementitious
> Husk & Covering, into Vacuum evaporating, revealing the lineaments of Man
> . . . rejoicing in Unity
> In the Four Senses, in the Outline, the Circumference, & Form, for ever . . .
>
> (*Jerusalem*)

Shirazeh Houshiary's wood, plaster, clay and straw pieces of 1982–3 came to life when mould grew in the clay and straw giving the works an animate, almost comic presence. They are not unfriendly beasts. Their inspiration is Persian poetry, but their form is oddly familiar to a Western sensibility. While their material presence is earthy and unthreatening (unlike Kapoor's), their holed, armed and leggy bodies are apparitions made flesh. Like Kapoor's, each piece is magnetically drawn to another like stars in a constellation. They have precedents in Barry Flanagan's sand and hessian aberrant, antediluvian forms of the sixties. They have origins in the dark ground of existence explored by the Surrealists. But Houshiary has beaten the Surrealists at their own game. She has put together the 'heads, bodies and tails' of The Exquisite Corpse.

Scratches, traces of bird's feet, of fossils, the nervous febrile arc of a wing, the imagery of Avis Newman's large drawings is that of an imaginary pre-linguistic world. Bird, animal and human forms predominate to give, as the artist says, 'tangible form to ancient feelings . . . to suggest the mobility of the image and that ambiguity of form which one experiences in dreams'. Her drawing, in charcoal, ink and graphite with its split and broken marks, its dark centres like wounds, expresses the deep fear of omnipresent death. Their screaming discord is emphasized by the works' titles: *Only the Beginnings of Terror, Rage on Death*. Essential to the artist's work is the act of drawing which Avis Newman considers a discursive practice, parallel to that of the novel, of poetry, of psychoanalysis. She purposefully rejects the conventional approaches to painting. Often she pieces together fragments to achieve an epic scale, and works around the edge of the canvas to avoid the centre as a starting point. By leaving the spaces open and the work not closed, not autonomous, she evokes association and invites response.

Alastair MacLennan's twelve-hour performance and installation, *Birth Death Day*, attempted to evoke a psychological and physical awareness of a primal sense of being in his audience. MacLennan, black garbed and blackened from head to foot, moved through the environment he created – a silent temple with the objects of ritual: dead fish, pigs' feet, tails and ears, circles of blood, cups of water, the pungent odour of decay – like a figure from the underworld ritually marking time, making time palpable. MacLennan, like Avis Newman, attempts to recover a pre-symbolic world.

Jo Baer and Bruce Robbins have worked collaboratively since 1978. Up to that time Jo Baer worked as a Minimalist painter and Bruce Robbins was a Conceptual artist. Both artists trained and worked earlier in the human sciences: Robbins as an anthropologist and Baer as a physiological psychologist working on perception theory. Their images – animals, birds, fish, the human female – are like actors in myth but there is no narrative, no anecdotal content. Baer and Robbins are not interested in Surrealist notions of automatic drawing or in the deep inner space of Surrealist painting. As far as possible their images are appropriated – from photographs or from other works – and traced. The artists are not involved in drawing as a virtuoso performance, but, like Deacon, in its essential role as *boundary*. The pale colour of Jo Baer's *Cleaving Apart/Together* takes on strength through the erotic nature of the image. The falling birds of Bruce Robbins's painting *The Snatcher* convey a sense of foreboding, of primeval history or *Urgeschichte*.[4]

In 1946 the sky – immaterial space – gave Yves Klein his all-blue monochrome paintings and in 1960 his one-note *Symphonie Monotone*. The monochrome, the primary structure, has never totally freed itself of a metaphysical vein. In doing away with gesture, with subjective artistic personality, it allows an unimpeded relationship between the work and the viewer. The minimalist ethos remains 'as nothing less than a kind of Rosetta stone for our age, the significance of whose code has not really been broken'.[5]

Alan Charlton is Britain's most consistent and most militant Minimal artist. Like Ad Reinhardt, the American painter, Charlton might well be described as the 'Great Demurer in a time of Great Enthusiasm'.[6] Reinhardt defined Fine Art as 'exclusive, negative, absolute and timeless'. Like him, Charlton 'avoids effusion by stating only what his art is not; it is not coloured, not composed, not inflected, not meaningful in any directly interpretable sense'.[7] But Charlton's work in installation has a presence which is at odds with its seeming nihilism. The paintings do not overwhelm or engulf through sheer size – their scale is human. Their *tabula rasa* presents an absence waiting to be filled.

John Carter spent a year in Italy in 1963–4. Pisan and Florentine architecture with its crystalline beauty, its clarity, had a strong impact: 'it was to do with colour and the structure coming into being at the same time'.[8] Carter has never seen his structures as more than 'the mildest extension of painting', the outcome of necessity for 'some kind of dialogue between painting and sculpture because of my need to somehow make painting more "real", as real as a building'. But while the constructivists broke with the plane, the flat surface, John Carter's works must be viewed frontally, like paintings on canvas. From the late seventies the artist has shifted from incorporating several elements into his structures to making one point, simply stated. It would be a mistake to underestimate the complexity of the decisions necessary to achieve such plain speaking. The directness of recent work echoes the steadfast gaze of a peasant madonna by Piero della Francesca. Piero was long regarded as a primitive, too barbaric for civilized taste, but for the twentieth century he revealed 'the family of things . . . the poetry of deep affinities'.[9]

Peter Joseph's interests in poetry, philosophy and music – especially of the early nineteenth century – are indivisible from his painting, which is a powerful synthesis of the Classical and the Romantic. His 1983 Chicago retrospective catalogue was prefaced with John Donne's words beginning, 'In all philosophy there is not so darke a thing as *light*. . .' Joseph, like Claude and Turner before him, is concerned with this most primordial of elements and its expression through colour. His works are long in the making, painted after a process of critical decision-making: on scale, on proportion and on colours used. Joseph intends the work to be finally realized within the experience of the viewer: 'The aspiration is to find that moment when feeling is not just emotional expression, but is transformed into value.'

Bob Law's interests in metaphysics, alchemy and mysticism have long been reflected in his work. He made his early black 'field' paintings of the sixties after lying in fields being aware 'of nature itself and my position in nature on earth'.[10] He has likened his work to the first Palaeolithic cave paintings and in 1964 wrote *The Necessity for Magic in Art*. This synthesis of nature philosophy, primitive art and oriental mysticism is indicated by his title for the black paintings: *Twentieth Century Icons*; he thought of them 'as having no beginning and no end; the complete object'. The absolute severity of Bob Law's personal search for 'the ever elusive truth' (he destroyed much of his earlier work) has the intensity of religious conviction. It redeems his negative vision: 'with our bits and pieces we can construct, *purely intuitively*, toward and around those elusive and treasured seconds when we feel sublimely elevated'.[11]

MARJORIE ALLTHORPE-GUYTON

NOTES

1 Newman's essays, 'The first man was an artist' and 'The sublime is now' (*Tigers Eye*, Oct. 1947 and Dec. 1948) focus on ideas which are as current now as then: the primacy of the aesthetic act, the necessity for dream, man's helplessness before the 'void'. It remains to be seen whether the recent shift towards resisting concepts of 'substance' and 'essence' in art, as argued by, notably, Jacques Derrida (*La Vérité en peinture*, Flammarion, Paris, 1978) will change these deep-rooted ideas.

2 Raymond Williams, *Keywords*, Fontana, London, 1983: 'alienation', p.34.

3 Wilhelm Worringer, *Abstraction and Empathy*, trans. M. Bullock, Routledge & Kegan Paul, London, 1963.

4 A term used by the German philosopher Walter Benjamin in his attempt to devise a 'science of the origin'.

5 Suzi Gablik, 'Minimalism' (1980), in *Concepts of Modern Art*, ed. Nikos Stangos, Thames & Hudson, London, 1981, p.253.

6 Lucy Lippard, 'The cult of the direct and the difficult', from the exhibition catalogue *Two Decades of American Painting*, Museum of Modern Art, New York, 1966–7, reprinted in *Changing. Essays in Art Criticism*, Dutton, New York, 1971, p.118.

7 ibid., p.116.

8 John Carter, conversation with Bryan Robertson, published in the catalogue of the artist's exhibition, Warwick Arts Trust, 1983.

9 Adrian Stokes, *Art and Science, A Study of Alberti, Piero della Francesca and Giorgione*, Faber & Faber, London, 1949, p. 36.

10 Conversation with Richard Cork, 1974, in 'Bob Law: A Chronology, 1958', prepared by Sandy Nairne for *Bob Law: Paintings and Drawings 1959–78*, Whitechapel Art Gallery, London, 1978.

11 Bob Law, *The Necessity for Magic in Art*, unpublished lecture, 1964.

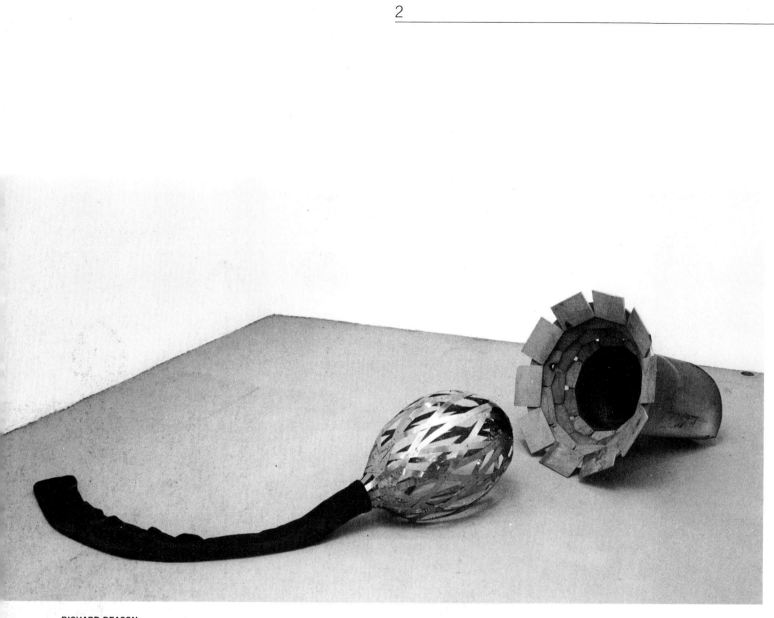

RICHARD DEACON
THE EYE HAS IT
1984
wood, galvanized steel, stainless
steel, brass and cloth
80 x 345 x 170 cm

SHIRAZEH HOUSHIARY
FIRE STOLEN BY BIRD
1981
7 objects: clay and wood
varying heights: from 61 to 137 cm

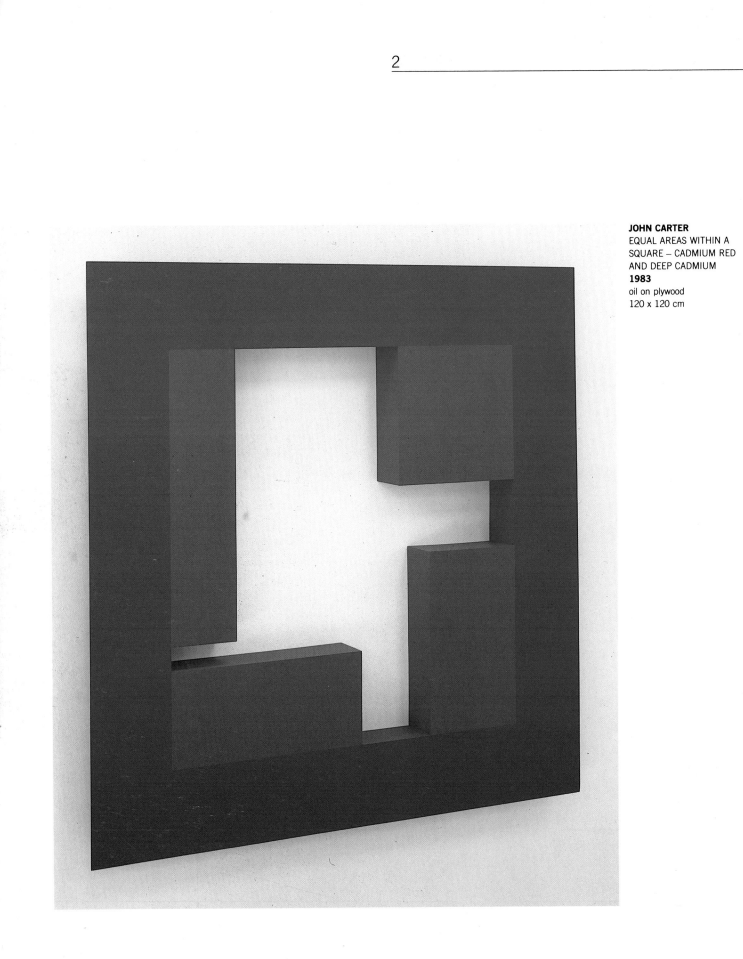

JOHN CARTER
EQUAL AREAS WITHIN A
SQUARE – CADMIUM RED
AND DEEP CADMIUM
1983
oil on plywood
120 x 120 cm

ANISH KAPOOR
INSTALLATION OF WORKS
IN ARTIST'S STUDIO
1984
polystyrene, cement, earth,
acrylic medium, pigment

ALASTAIR MacLENNAN
CLEAN SWEEP
1981
7½-hour non-stop performance
Triskel Arts Centre,
Cork, Southern Ireland

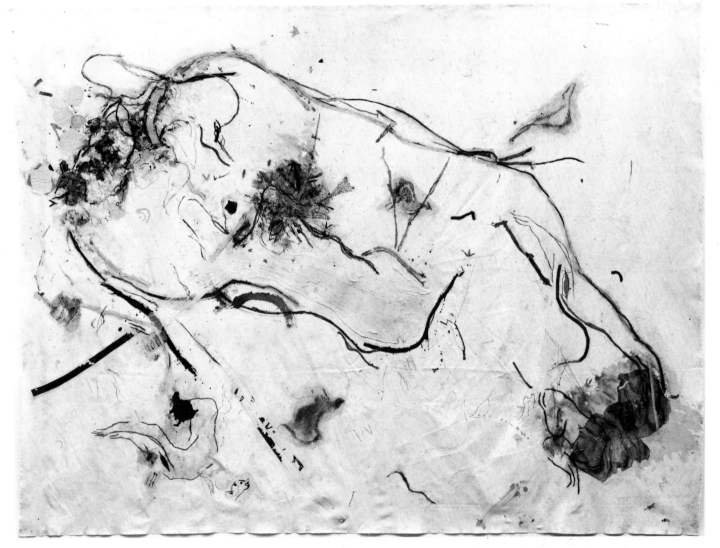

AVIS NEWMAN
THIS . . . THE DREAM'S NAVEL
1983-4
two-part piece:
mixed media on canvas
274.3 x 366 cm
boxed book – steel box
and lithograph on paper
50.8 x 39.4 cm

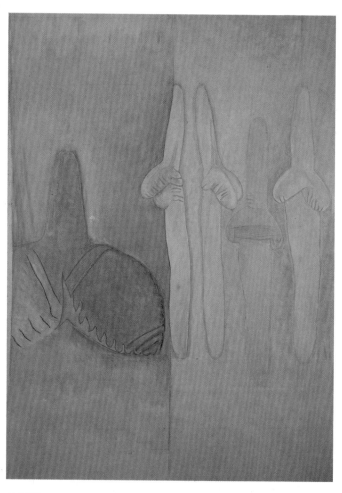

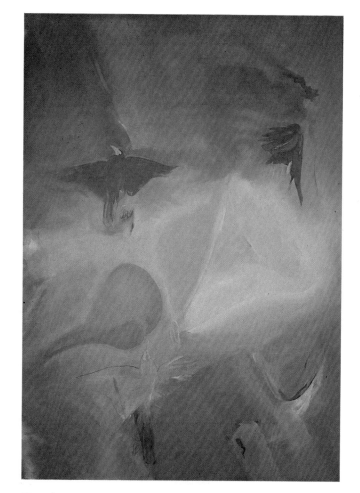

JO BAER
CLEAVING (APART/TOGETHER)
1979
oil on canvas
213.4 x 152.4 cm

BRUCE ROBBINS
THE SNATCHER
(THE COLLECTOR OF GENITALS)
1981
oil on canvas
243.8 x 183 cm

PETER JOSEPH
ROSE WITH BROWN SURROUND
FEBRUARY 1983
acrylic on cotton duck
157 x 153 cm

BOB LAW
VINCENT'S CHAIR
1984
painted wood
90 x 46 x 45 cm

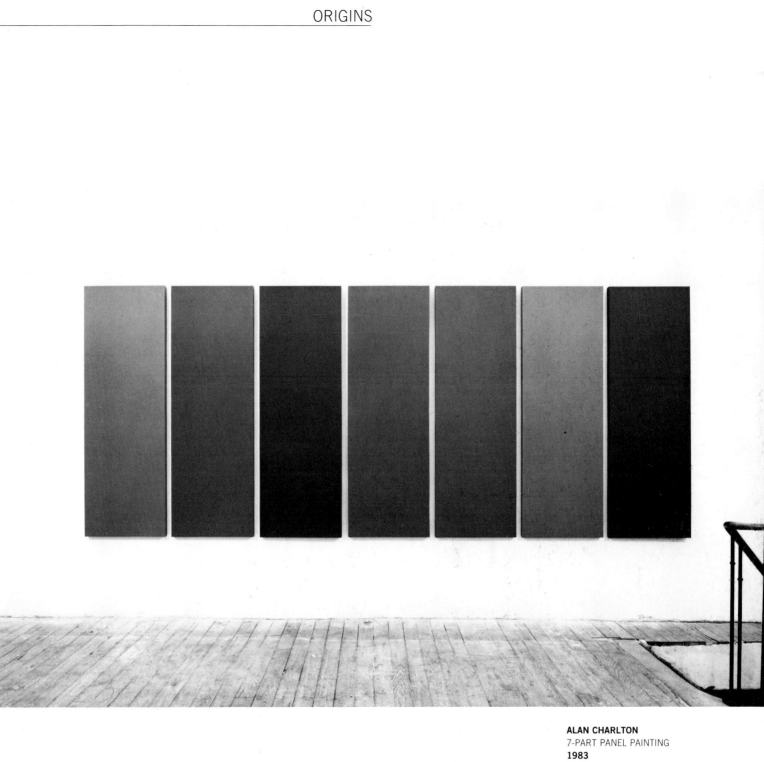

ALAN CHARLTON
7-PART PANEL PAINTING
1983
installation: Durand-Dessert
Gallery, Paris November 1983
acrylic on cotton duck
180 x 447 cm
(not in exhibition)

CRITICAL ATTITUDES

Lenin's view that criticism is always a social act is well known: the critic has a position and a role – situated within society, he or she speaks on society's behalf at the same time as criticizing its condition. The position of the artist as critic, although not exclusively a modern phenomenon – one thinks of Brueghel, Hogarth and others – is integral to the theory of 'vanguardism', deriving, as it must, from a stance of continual self-assessment. The modernist spirit of criticism can be seen at work in all the manifestoes of the early avant-garde movements – those of Futurism, Dada and Surrealism – and in the writings of poet-critics like Marinetti, Tzara and Breton. Its more inward-looking aspect explored ways of reflecting upon the state of art itself, of ensuring 'continuous' revolution in language and style. Its other concern was to establish a distance between the values which governed the work of the avant-garde and those that prevailed in society at large; in other words, to emphasize their acceptance of the 'revolutionary' principles of 'vanguardism' in opposition to bourgeois life styles and bourgeois culture. Such artists and writers saw themselves as irritants to the settled political structure of religion and class. Their critical gaze sought to achieve what has been termed an 'agonistic'[1] relationship with the social and political status quo. However, the 'agonism' of these early vanguard movements served merely to reconsecrate the Romantic cult of the unique, creative individual, fatally embroiled with a deterministic view of the future.

The intelligent bourgeois's disgust with the complacency of bourgeois society and the argument for the destruction of social institutions and social relations, which asserted the bourgeois creed of individual freedom in its most essential form, are demonstrated by André Breton's 'Prolegomena' to the third Surrealist manifesto, written in 1942.[2] After setting down a prophetic programme for social reform, Breton plunges into artistic self-indulgence. After rejecting the idea of 'party' discipline, he goes on to underline the bourgeois anarchist notion of freedom: 'Man must be absolutely convinced that once there has been general consent on a given subject, individual resistance is the only key to the prison.' When Breton wrote his introduction to the third manifesto, in the middle of the Second World War, he was already beset with fears that international Marxism would not be able to deliver the new social order. Nevertheless, the dilemma he expressed and the manner in which it was posed remain relevant for the critically inclined or politically committed artist of today. The freedom to make judgments unfettered by 'rules and agreements', to 'search for the Golden Fleece all by oneself', and never to be reconciled with the 'unanimous vote of an assembly that will not take it upon itself to contradict a larger assembly', forms the irreducible basis of the modern artist's credo.

Whenever vanguardist art movements have allied themselves with the struggle of the proletariat, although their declared aims might be progressive and egalitarian, the precedence given to the needs of the individual before the demands of social relations has generated a powerful odour of condescension. Driven by self-disgust, the bourgeois revolutionary urge to transform society is not, as Marx and Engels pointed out in the *Communist Manifesto* of 1848, 'genuinely evolutionary'. It is both prescriptive and power-seeking. It puts an end to 'all feudal, patriarchal, idyllic relations' and leaves 'no other nexus between man and man than naked self-interest'. Nor is it against capital as such; it seeks rather to gain access to it for its own ends. The development of the art market, in tandem with the revolutionary progress of the Modern Movement, might be said to embody this process. By usurping the position of the academies as professionally competent, value-setting institutions, the commercial demands and values of the market place have dissolved the long-standing ties which bound artists to patrons. A new, quasi-social structure was perfected – the gallery system. The artist has become a producer of goods; the buyer, a consumer. Between the two, the dealer – a new kind of expert – functions as a manipulator according to the bourgeois conception of property. 'Social relation' is thus replaced by 'property relation'.

Rejection of the old social formulation of art, coupled with the modern artists' insistence that the work of art is first a 'reification' – a manifestation – of the complex personality of the artist, have conspired with the forces of commerce to make art increasingly marginal to the needs of society. In Britain, the most systematic and highly theorized examination of this rupture has been pursued by those who have worked in and around a group of artists using the collective title Art & Language. The group, rooted in the Conceptual Art movement of the early seventies, addresses itself to 'technical' and 'philosophical' questions regarding the relationship of language to art. There are three aspects to these artists' approach: first, working collectively, they challenge the Romantic, modernist view that works of art are projections of an individual sensibility; and, by the form that the work takes, they question, second, the assumption that art is of necessity 'visual'; and, third, that its life is best expressed in the form of objects. Their assault upon the object-based conception of the work of art is as fundamental and far-reaching as that implied by Marcel Duchamp's 'readymades'. Where they differ from Duchamp is in working to a clear 'political' objective. Art & Language's challenge is directed at the art market – at its capacity to mediate the most uncompromising actions and utterances of the artist in terms of 'property value'. Beyond this, they seek to bypass all conventional forms of judgment. For them the language of art must be genuinely democratic and open, its reading the prerogative of no particular coterie or social class.

Viewed from the outside, Terry Atkinson's departure from the Art & Language group in 1975 signalled not so much a disagreement with broad critical objectives as an unease over critical method.[3] Where Art & Language, by employing a teleological approach to the objects, values and processes of art, were developing a socio-political perspective at one remove within the context of art, Atkinson wanted a more direct relation between his practice as an artist and his politics. His critical address is directed first of all, then, to 'late capitalist society' as the background against which all western art is made and seen. In this respect he is both artist-critic and political satirist, bent on exposing the hypocrisy in what is generally accepted as the relationship between the art world and social life. Atkinson's approach is shared by John Hyatt, who employs a similar kind of 'punning' pictorialization in which literary devices are used to radicalize the image, and images are used to disrupt the logical flow of written language. Atkinson and Hyatt allow image and word to come together to form a 'picture', and this is where they part company with Art & Language.

The rebirth of interest in picture making is perhaps the most radical characteristic of post-Modernist art. Pictorial representation speaks of common experience. It follows, therefore, that no matter how curiously coloured a particular representation might be it reflects a generally recognized 'social ordering'. By shifting attention away from the 'thing itself' and on to 'what is being depicted' it represents the re-establishing of the 'social' dimension at the centre of contemporary art practice. The possibilities which a return to pictorial rhetoric have opened up can be observed in artists as seemingly diverse as John Yeadon, Jock McFadyen, Terry Setch, Graham Durward, Bill Woodrow and Stephen McKenna. Yeadon and McFadyen both reveal an interest in political and social reportage – semi-autobiographical with a hard ideological edge. Setch's politics are less to the fore, but, by his use of materials to make metaphors of environmental decay, his pictures never fail to invoke a strong sense of social, perhaps even moral, decline. The same theme is picked up by Durward and by Woodrow. Durward is very much the neo-Expressionist: the first attack is on the sensibility, leaving no refuge in comfortable aesthetic contemplation. Woodrow is the strategist: his transformations of common-or-garden objects amount to a form of legerdemain through which familiar relationships are converted into powerful symbols of futility, oppression and violence.

At first sight, McKenna's work appears to be very different. He deals with no overtly political or even topical subject, and his obvious attachment to the canons of 'great painting' might seem to set him aside in some curious mannerist backwater. Yet he mounts, in the most subtly telling way, a critique which is central to the Post-Modernist debate. By insisting that the continuing social and cultural life of painting subsists in the tradition of pictorial crafts, he asks important questions of the modernist construction of history – its reification of the idea of progress. His central attack, then, is directed at modernist 'historicism'.

Like McKenna, Ian Hamilton Finlay is also concerned to develop a 'correct' view of history – in his case through a theory of language. Finlay's 'new classicism' defines language as a neutral system of symbols which become expressive or depictive only in the context of social relations – as part of social exchange – and so embodies a very particular view of cultural history as distinct from political history. The cultural records the continuous reinterpretation of those things which are fundamentally unchanging and unchangeable, while the political maps the all too human struggle to change and perfect the practical circumstances of life. The forcing of this distinction allows Finlay to disassociate himself from the bourgeois rejection of culture which lies at the heart of the Modern Movement.

If a renewed interest in 'picturing' represents one important critical response to the impasse of Modernism, then the turning away from the traditional mediums of painting and sculpture presents another very different response. Installation work, performance art and the use of photography and video constitute a search for more socially accessible forms of art practice. At their most critical they generate their force by working from or against the trappings of high capitalist culture. For artists like Victor Burgin, Tim Head, Rose Finn-Kelcey, Kevin Atherton and, to a lesser extent, Gerald Newman, reference to a world dominated by both the media and the mediated image is not only essential for the making of their work, but also for its readability. Burgin, for instance, focuses our attention on the use of the photographic image in advertising. His critical method reveals the hidden mechanism, which underlies the effective- ness of the image as a mirror for human desire. By parodying the highly polished visual clichés of advertising, he causes us to reflect on its function as fetishizer of social roles, character types and consumer products. In Tim Head's work it is the man-made environment which is the subject of our critical gaze. By means of a semiotic reading of architecture and the design of consumer products he connects the materialist urban world with extreme forms of social violence and shows it voicing back its inner destructive forces. Rose Finn-Kelcey also treats of violence. For her, war can only be understood in terms of particular socio-political concepts – for example, competition, heroism, nationalism, cultural chauvinism – which are, in their turn, rooted in the way the media project ideas and figures of authority. Kevin Atherton draws attention to the alienating effect of television, pointing to the way it isolates the individual, elicits a stereotyped response and frustrates the need for social exchange. With these artists the critical approach is uncompromisingly direct; they openly employ the rhetorical tropes of a visual world which is familiar to all, but in the case of Newman we are presented with a more oblique view. Newman works exclusively with sound – processing gleanings from newspaper reportage, using 'scratch' recordings as well as original scripted material. The subject matter often refers to breakdowns in social morality, as, for instance, gratuitous acts of corporate violence. For Newman, whose working process is slow and painstaking, the need to realize his material in the form of a highly aestheticized experience is paramount.

Bruce McLean's involvement with performance dates from the sixties, and remains the core of everything he does. His paintings are traces of physical actions; likewise his sculptures which lie in awkward repose, evidence of a frenetic assault upon stone. The main thrust of his approach to making seems to be 'to do and to do quickly'. The moment of freedom which allows him to act has to be snatched at – if missed it is lost irretrievably. McLean's theme then is the elusiveness of true (i.e. unconditioned) experience, which he explored first in 1972 with his 'pose band' called 'Nice Style'. 'Pose' satirically referred to the artificiality of the art world, formed out of clichéd preconceptions of every kind – social, political and economic as well as aesthetic. Within such a world, the role conferred on the artist spelt for McLean the end of the artist's freedom to think and act independently. 'Pose' demonstrates the negation of expressive purpose, and functions therefore as a metaphor of imprisonment with implications for society at large. In the later paintings and sculptures he escapes this imprisonment by holding on to the moment of action in which freedom is consecrated in the life of the mark.

Stuart Brisley is concerned with the dilemmas involved in personal freedom, but unlike McLean his view is coloured by existential despair. In the early performance works, he adopted the classic avant-garde method of establishing a confrontational relationship with his audience. He became unpoliticized man – unwitting victim and oppressor, blind to social relations, careless of human need, motivated by pressing self-interest. In a black and airless environment, which reflected his socially deprived state, he endlessly rehearsed actions and gestures conveying a growing sense of futility. The same concerns inform his recent sculptures but his method is no longer confrontational. Their architecture is stubbornly inexpressive and functions as a container for gestures and actions which have no discernible connection with human motivation and desire, signifying life on the edge of non-life. In Brisley's work it is possible to read sculptural structure as a metaphor for a social structure in which the urgent human need to communicate is held in a perpetual state of unfulfilment. Brisley points directly to what is perhaps the most important underlying preoccupation of all politically inclined artists – the position allowed to the individual by the society in which he or she lives where this is characterized as the gift of social and economic freedom: with artists like Atkinson, Hyatt, McFadyen and Yeadon, he seeks to expose its consequences for social life in general.

JON THOMPSON

NOTES

1 The realization of a state of conflict – in this case between the artist and the society in which the artist works – has an important spiritual dimension, which Mario Praz called a state of 'romantic agony'. It is therefore characterized by 'tragic heroism'. See R. Poggioli, *The Theory of the Avant Garde*, Harvard University Press, Cambridge, Mass., 1968.

2 The third Surrealist manifesto commenced by Breton in 1942. Only the introduction, the 'Prolegomena', was completed.

3 Terry Atkinson was a founder member of the Art & Language group. He parted company with them in 1975.

STEPHEN McKENNA
O, ILIUM!
1982
oil on canvas
180 x 250 cm

BRUCE McLEAN
SCOTTISH HAT AND SWORD
DANCE
1982
acrylic and chalk on cotton
3 parts, each: 280 x 150 cm
overall size: 280 x 450 cm

TIM HEAD
STATE OF THE ART
1984
colour photograph
183 x 274 cm

VICTOR BURGIN
from GRADIVA
1982
No. 3 in a series of black and white
photographs
each 50.8 x 61cm

JOHN HYATT
ART, WARS, DIVISION
AND DESIGN
JUNE-AUGUST 1982
oil, housepaint and
carspray on canvas
124.5 x 266.7 cm

TERRY ATKINSON
IDEOLOGICALLY BATTERED
POSTCARD FROM TROTSKY
IN COYOACAN
TO STALIN IN MOSCOW,
DATED 1938
1981-2
mixed media
269 x 201 cm

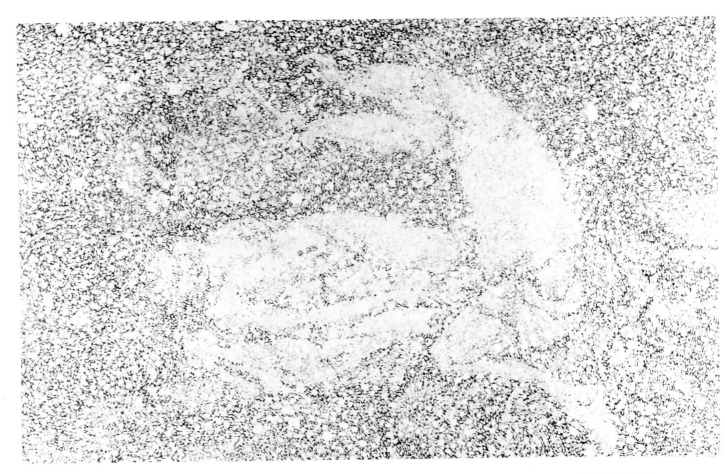

ART & LANGUAGE
STUDY FOR IMPRESSIONISM
RETURNING SOME TIME
IN THE FUTURE
1984
acrylic paint on paper
107 x 168 cm
(not in exhibition)

IAN HAMILTON FINLAY
NAMES ON TREES/
PLAQUES ON TREES
1984
2 of 10 plaques at the Merian
Park, Basel, Switzerland with
Nicholas Sloan
(not in exhibition)

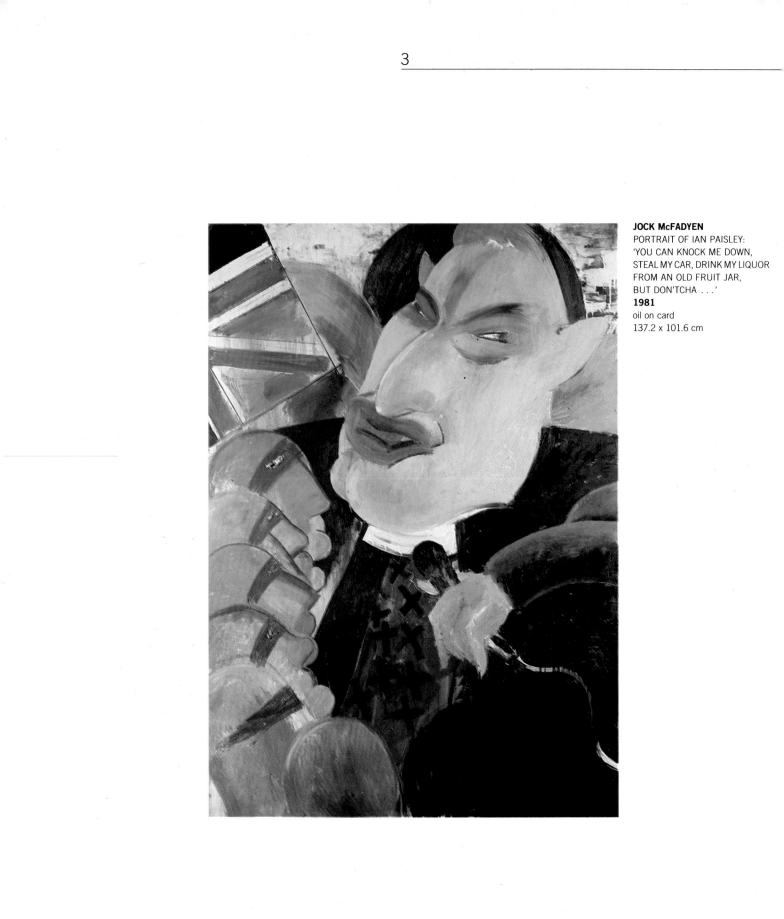

JOCK McFADYEN
PORTRAIT OF IAN PAISLEY:
'YOU CAN KNOCK ME DOWN,
STEAL MY CAR, DRINK MY LIQUOR
FROM AN OLD FRUIT JAR,
BUT DON'TCHA . . .'
1981
oil on card
137.2 x 101.6 cm

JOHN YEADON
MIDNIGHT ON FREEDOM
(BRITAINIA STREET WALTZ)
1982
acrylic on canvas
183 x 213 cm

GRAHAM DURWARD
FIRST CRIME IN THE FOREST
1984
oil on canvas
198 x 319 cm

STUART BRISLEY
1 = 66,666
(GEORGIANA COLLECTION VI)
MARCH 1983
wood, steel, plaster, leather,
nylon, cloth and paper
217 x 500 x 81 cm

TERRY SETCH
TWO WOMEN, GREENHAM
JUNE 1984
encaustic wax and oil
on canvas
305 x 351 cm

BILL WOODROW
A PASSING CAR, A CARING WORD
1982
car door, double-bed base
244 x 152.4 x 244 cm

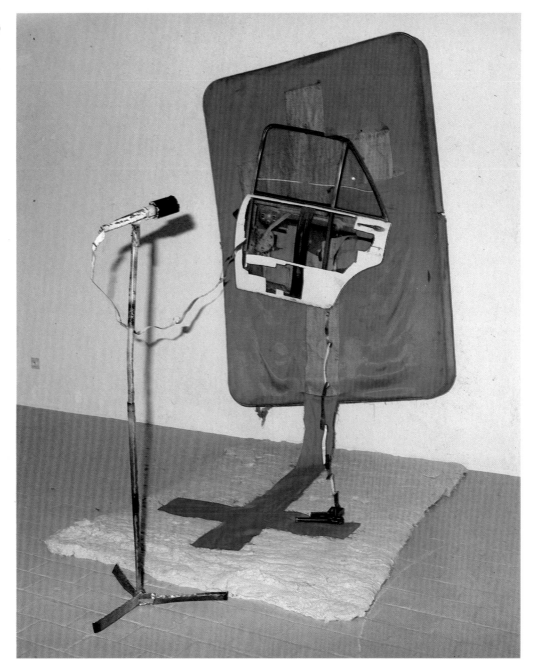

ROSE FINN-KELCEY
from GLORY
1983
colour videotape
20 minutes

SOUTH ATLANTIC

Zone – 19 mins

Epitaph – 9 mins

GERALD NEWMAN
SOUTH ATLANTIC
1982
(TIMES Nos. 14 & 15)
stereophonic tape recording
28 minutes

KEVIN ATHERTON
from VIDEO TIMES
1984
dual publication and video
installation
(not in exhibition)

VISUAL POETRY

There have been many most excellent Poets, that never versified.
(Sir Philip Sidney, *Apologia Poetica*)

Poetry asserts the ambiguities of words through the resonance of association. Used poetically, words have no fixed meaning; they are not counters of the mind but metaphors inwardly alive. Art can likewise use the strategies of poetic language which, Dr Johnson suggests, 'pleases by exhibiting an idea more grateful to the mind than things themselves'. The following artists recognize that art is just one of many languages in a linguistically pluralist society. For them art 'has become a mode, partly technical, partly ideological, of *experiencing* language'.[1] Unlike T. S. Eliot's J. Alfred Prufrock, who became exhausted by the quest, they have a sense of optimism — of hope for the renewed power of art to salvage and transform the fragmented relics of a dying culture, to re-till the wasteland. While some, perhaps Stephen Johnson, John Murphy and Tony Carter, would agree with Keats that the poet 'has no identity; he is continually informing and filling some other body', others are engaged by the notion of poetic identity, of the artist as hero or fool. A recent performance by Stephen Taylor Woodrow – 'poet, performance artist, avant-garde tap dancer' — was called with self-parodying irony 'The Budding Bard Blurts Out'. Steven Campbell and Michael Sandle might well also see themselves as bards – visionaries perched over the detritus of a fallen world. There is no doubt that British artists have increasingly appealed to a literary tradition in their search. This does not, however, guarantee that their work can be easily read; the interweaving of image/object and idea can be as complex, ambiguous and oblique as the elliptical syntax of James Joyce.

The idea of the artist as revealer rather than maker is central to the work of Richard Wentworth, Stephen Johnson, John Murphy and Tony Carter. Like Baudelaire, their 'poetic excitation' is sited at the 'interstices between image and idea, word and thing'.[2] They usually work with ready-made objects, from which an idea germinates very slowly until a key form or relationship is discovered which will allow construction of the work. When that point is reached, form and content become indivisible; the work makes itself through an inherent logic.

Richard Wentworth 'discovers' his sculptures after entering into long complicity with usually very mundane objects: a bucket, a lamp bulb, a paper bag, a pocket. A pocket . . . ? Wentworth found that it was possible to buy pockets – on their own. In pristine state, stitched and ready, they took on an absurd, a disarming and disturbing character quite unrelated to their original purpose. He is constantly intrigued at the way we use objects as 'a sort of sub-language . . . makeshift but intelligible'.[3] Like the rubber glove in which a friend threw down a bunch of keys, 'as it fell to earth it looked like a greeting or the hand of God smiting me from on high'.

Stephen Johnson's small sculpture *Cloud* connects with ideas about the currency of art which John Murphy also explored in his series *An Art of Exchange*. Johnson's *Stick minus Phosphorus (exorcism)* and *Wish Fulfilment* where each 'flower' has been transformed from a coin of the realm, annealed, beaten and burnished, lucidly express the notion of altered states. They might have been accompanied by the alchemical text which John Murphy used for his work *Pyromenon* (product of fire): 'art in imitation of nature opens a body by means of fire but uses a much stronger fire than the fire that is produced by the fire of the confined flame'.[4] These words, juxtaposing generative, intellectual energy with sexual energy, are an apt metaphor for Murphy's latest paintings. *The Gathering Anguish Strikes Beneath* is the severest of things: its meticulous presentation and execution effects a distancing, a feeling of something beyond touch, not palpable. It is erotic; a fantasy, not an encounter.

Tony Carter likewise attempts to unite sensual and intellectual pleasure. He honours the intrinsic nature of his objects: he may alter their surfaces but he does not turn them into something else. It is as if he peels away one layer of reality to reveal another. He makes not another version of familiar things – a knife, a saucepan, a photograph – but an after-image, a ghost heavy with association, 'mixing memory and desire'.[5] Like Murphy he takes obsessive care with the process of making and with the titles – equivalences – for the final works: 'a thought is more valuable the more it reflects process and the emergence of unexpected forms'.[6] The richly organic imagery, like *A Midsummer Night's Dream* fantasy, of *Virus – of War and Subjective Seeing* is at odds with the grim, political reality of the event – a news picture of refugees fleeing from Bangladesh. In *Virus* he repainted in oil part of an enlarged photograph of his earlier work *Elysium for Newsprint Distortions,* seeing his intervention as an insidious invasion, a disease-like war, an aberrant form of life.

In a letter of 1809 Goethe wrote: 'That fig tree, this little snake, the chrysallis lying there in front of the window quietly awaiting the future – all these are pregnant with meaning. Indeed, anyone who knew how to decipher them properly would soon be able to do without all writing and speech.'[7] With the magical touch of juggling metaphorists, Alison Wilding and Barry Flanagan reveal meaning in objects through a direct physical engagement with material. Alison Wilding takes the most unexpected object such as a paper cup, gives it a history, and it is a token, a talisman. Her forms are often animal – a wing, a beak – but like Flanagan there is often an allusion to the human and the human-made. Her dialogue with material – copper, brass, wood and stone – is prolonged and meditative, and the works have an inherent sense of time past – of quiescent 'closeness and farness', words inscribed by Flanagan on one of his drawings.

A lightness and flexibility of thought coupled with an iconoclastic disregard for conventions give Barry Flanagan's work a fecund élan which seems as natural to him as leaves to a tree. His lithe, agile hares – on bell, anvil, cricket stumps or simply boxing – expose not only the absurd in man and his false identities, but his courage in the face of an incomprehensible world. The rich language of Flanagan's sculpture, and his roving but deft use of materials – hessian, rope, sand, stone, bronze and clay – recall both the free-wheeling burlesque of the absurd drama and poetry of Alfred Jarry and Beckett and the elliptical, fragmented conjunctions of concrete poetry. It 'poses a theory of art as play, of verse as a sort of verbal nursery',[8] and Flanagan, like Ian Hamilton Finlay in some of his poem sculptures, is a player of word and image. His drawings and sculptures are a lexicon of emblems which he makes into performers. He said, 'poetry is the most economical manifestation of one's "chemistry" – always working towards poem'.[9] Horace said, 'painters and poets alike have always had licence to dare anything', and Flanagan, unlike Eliot's Prufrock, 'dares to disturb the universe'.

Steven Campbell's *The building accuses the architect of bad design* evokes the disturbed states of that reality beneath the surface which Dostoevsky, Kafka and Joyce explored in their congested poetic imagery. Like Joyce's Stephen Dedalus, Campbell's thick-bodied, neckless young man stumbles through an alien, hostile world; he is weighted down by heavy hikers' boots and absurdly impractical clothes. His boots, his body, are as much metaphors for his slavery to the absurd condition of his quest as Stephen Taylor Woodrow's *Triptych Man* is a prisoner of his triple identity. The landscape is threatening: it represents a dangerous world to be encountered with caution, not engaged on equal terms. Campbell's plants, rocks and trees are in a constant state of metamorphosis while his alter ego is as likely to change shape as Billy Bunter.

This inability to fix the dynamic state of nature, to engage in its activity is what Ian McKeever seeks to confront in *Beside the brambled ditch*. His cross-referencing among the cultural activities of painting, drawing, photography and the natural processes of the landscape essentially follows a Faustian principle: the only ethical path for man is to find and explore what exists. The recent *Night Flak* series originated from a reading of the German Romantic poet Novalis's six odes on death, *Hymnen an die Nacht*. The works were painted in the dark, and the artist found his perception of colour was heightened rather than diminished, confirming Goethe's conviction that apparent conflict can enhance experience. McKeever would aspire, like Constable, to be a 'natural painter', more interested in the geophysical than the metaphysical.

Like Campbell, both John Davies and Adrian Wiszniewski are preoccupied with a loss of sense and of identity. John Davies's black, dense drawing of a man behind bars is Camus's *L'Etranger*, alone and condemned. His heads and male figures are rarely recognizable as portraits; their streaked, lined and grey pallor gives them the presence of effigies – of now remote but once real individuals. Grouped *en masse*, they are an anthropological collection, a family of mankind, yet remote from each other. Wiszniewski's *My Jewish brother* evokes a narcissistic melancholy and a poetic alienation. He seems to dwell in true Romantic vein on those twin evils of the modern world: industrialization and materialist secularism. His poet heroes are embellished by the rich Baroque tradition of Polish folk art and by inventive allusions to Picasso's poetic allegory of the *Minotaur*; a darker world even than Keats's *Endymion*:

> how crude and sore
> The journey homeward to habitual self

Thérèse Oulton, Michael Sandle and Peter Bailey indicate an expression unusual to British art. While there is a powerful tradition of the cosmic epic in British literature from Milton to Joyce's *Ulysses*, the British artist, with the notable exceptions of Blake, Turner and John Martin, has never been much at home with the eschatological dimension of myth.

The paintings of Thérèse Oulton are heroically ambitious, engaging in a painterly discourse with Turner and in a poetic dialogue with the French symbolist painter Gustav Moreau. Her work, with its mythic references, for example to Orpheus in *Old gold*, reveals her interest in exploring the labyrinth of art history and her own cultural roots. It is a similar journey to that which Stephen McKenna has turned into a strenuous critical campaign.

Michael Sandle looks back to the apocalyptic paintings of Turner, to the fallacy of hope of Géricault's *Raft of the Medusa* and the sado-masochism of Delacroix's *Death of Sardanapalus*. Sandle's sculpture is a paradigm of futility. He takes the forms in which we dress up death – the catafalque, the tomb – but lays bare the reality of corrupted flesh. There is an ambiguity in the monumental, heroic scale of his work and ideas, which reflects a paradox in the contemporary psyche: the persistent aggrandizement and aesthetic ritualizing of war and its technology. Sandle straddles a knife edge between a positive and negative vision; like Nietzsche, he is aware that 'if you gaze for long into an abyss, the abyss gazes also into you'.

In Peter Bailey's Dantesque parodies there is a kaleidoscope of symbolic imagery often humorously interwoven with mythical references. In *Daphne and Apollo (an attempted rape)* dismembered dolls are the *memento mori* of a culture which refuses to recognize its physical and spiritual limitations. Bailey garners the detritus of nature and culture – dead cats to Cindy dolls and Action man – which he uses, like Jonathan Swift, as 'Th'artillery of words' to focus satire on a grotesque world.

A sense of decay and corruption in the modern world, intrinsic to the poetry of Baudelaire, Huysman and Eliot, is evoked, without rhetoric but with astringent wit, by Gareth Fisher. From plaster, plastic and wrought iron, he fashions sculptures which are tragi-comic parodies of contemporary values. *Sprouting head*, *Flag* and *Torso* present a *danse macabre* of Western culture.

Station House Opera's performances reverse the order of things; they turn the world on its head. In *Sex & Death* 'normality' was confounded when bodies and objects, all painted blue, turned into each other. *Drunken Madness*, a parody of bourgeois fantasy, also has a sting in its tail; like Dostoevsky's *Legend of the Grand Inquisitor* it is a savage indictment of the rationale of a society organized in the service of pleasure. One of the starting points for *Ultramundane* was the story of *The Garden of Forking Paths* by Jorge Luis Borges and, while these artists use literary sources, their language is that of a non-literary European tradition – of the comedian, of mime, cabaret and the circus. It develops from process and from the knowledge that the image – the language of performance – can violently usurp the supremacy of the text.

MARJORIE ALLTHORPE-GUYTON

NOTES

1 Jonathan Raban, *The Society of the Poem*, Harrap, London, 1971, p. 24.

2 Walter Benjamin, 'On some Motifs in Baudelaire', *Illuminations*, Fontana, London, 1982, p. 166.

3 Richard Wentworth, interview by Stuart Morgan, in *Richard Wentworth*, exhibition catalogue, Lisson Gallery, London, 1984.

4 The alchemical terms 'opening a body' and 'the fire of the confined flame' are metaphors for the sex act. See John Murphy, interview by Jon Thompson, *Aspects*, No. 9, winter 1979/80.

5 T. S. Eliot, *The Waste Land*, Faber & Faber, London, 1922.

6 Ernst Cassirer, *The Philosophy of the Enlightenment*, Beacon Press, Boston, 1965, p. 301.

7 To J.D. Falk; *Goethe on Art*, selected, edited and translated by John Gage, Scolar Press, London, 1980, p. 73.

8 Raban, op. cit., p. 111.

9 Barry Flanagan, quoted by Michael Compton in 'A Developing Practice', *Barry Flanagan*, exhibition catalogue, Whitechapel Art Gallery, London, 1982, p. 18.

RICHARD WENTWORTH
PYRE
1983/4
rubber and brass
38 x 38 x 38 cm
(not in exhibition)

ALISON WILDING
BLUEBLACK
1984
lime and elm woods, wax, lead
36 x 28 x 49 cm

TONY CARTER
VIRUS – OF WAR AND SUBJECTIVE
SEEING
1979-82
oil paint over photographic print,
3 easels, extended to
approx. 228.5 cm, 1 chair

JOHN MURPHY
THE GATHERING ANGUISH
STRIKES BENEATH
1982-3
oil on linen
185.4 x 144.8 cm

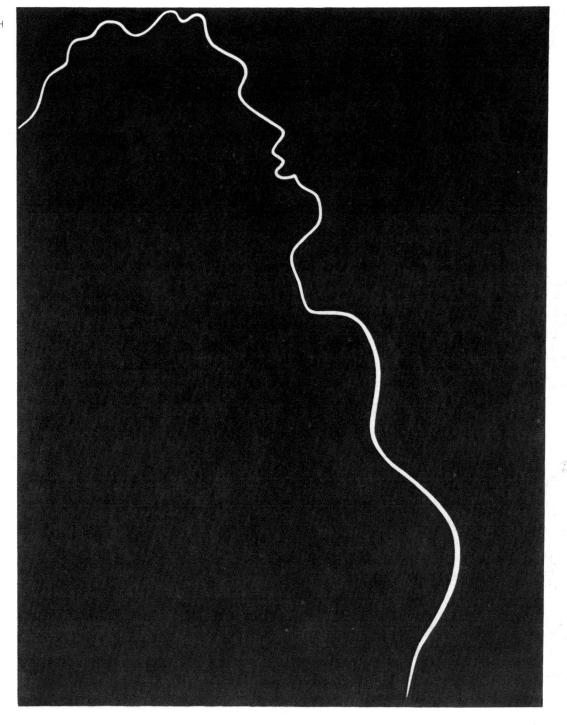

IAN McKEEVER
BESIDE THE BRAMBLED DITCH
1983
oil on photograph on canvas
230 x 208 cm

BARRY FLANAGAN
SOPRANO 1981 bronze No. 7
1981
bronze, partly gilded
80 x 66 x 57 cm

STEPHEN JOHNSON
CLOUD
1982
plated copper
7.6 cm high

JOHN DAVIES
THE ARTIST'S STUDIO
1984

ADRIAN WISZNIEWSKI
MY JEWISH BROTHER
1983-4
oil on canvas
182.9 x 243.8 cm

THÉRÈSE OULTON
OLD GOLD
1984
oil on canvas
205.7 x 259.1 cm

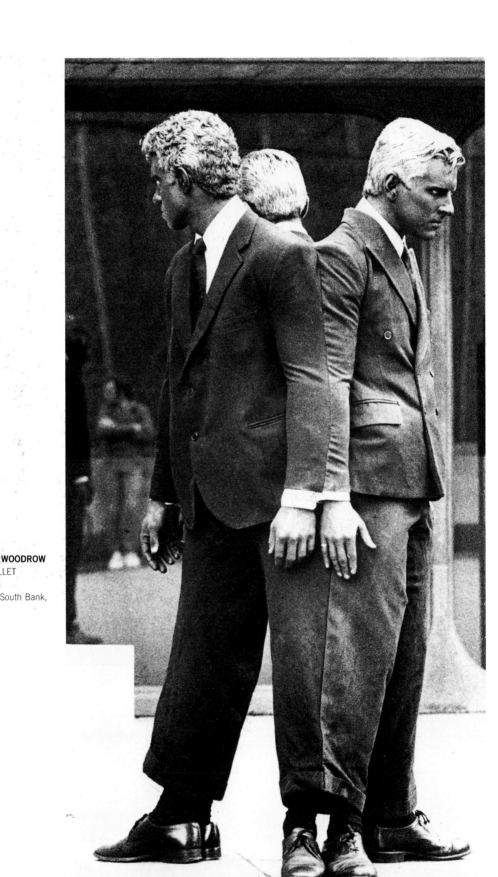

STEPHEN TAYLOR WOODROW
THE TRIPTYCH BALLET
first presented 1983
presentation on the South Bank,
London, 1984

STEVEN CAMPBELL
THE BUILDING ACCUSES THE
ARCHITECT OF BAD DESIGN
1984
oil on canvas
287 x 287 cm

PETER BAILEY
P.C.B. IN ISENHEIM
AND BUTETOWN
(A SATIRE AGAINST MARRIAGE)
1983
mixed media
238.8 x 167.6 x 12.7 cm

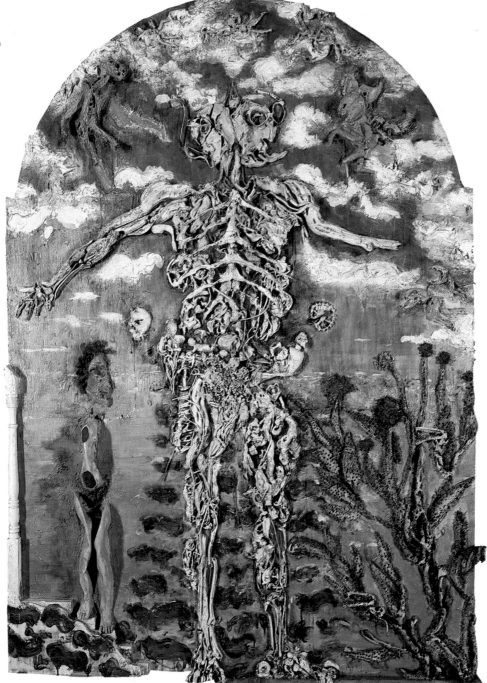

STATION HOUSE OPERA
SCENES FROM A NEW JERICHO
1984
performance on the South Bank,
London

GARETH FISHER
SPROUTING HEAD
1983
plaster and mixed media
45.7 x 25.4 x 25.4 cm

MICHAEL SANDLE
SECOND WORLD WAR MEMORIAL
1981
bronze, edition of 8
55 x 134 x 72 cm

SIGNS OF LANGUAGE

The Lord whose oracle is at Delphi neither speaks nor conceals: he gives signs. (Heraclitus)

Many artists of importance to the modern period have made 'procedure' or 'system' the central issue of their work. And yet to argue that any work of art is reducible to a mere procedure or system would be foolhardy. Even more artists have used a combination of the two as part of their working strategy. It would seem that there is an attraction in the distinct and recognizable quality of 'authenticity' that these disciplines bring. In so far as it sets the tone of the work as unquestionably modern, we might call this authenticity 'modernist', and we would not be far off the mark. Actually, it is more precisely located than such a term would imply. The very special notion of authenticity which a strong version of 'method' brings to the modernist work of art is connected, in general, with the sense of verity which artists since the middle of the nineteenth century have appropriated from modern science. In order to produce a sense of truth which has the appearance of being objective and 'concrete', artists in common with scientists have attempted the creation of non-metaphorical forms of language. This has led to work which shares some of the characteristics of scientific research: often 'propositional', it works to a programme, but one which is never seen as exhaustive in its scope; it deploys an 'objective' method which is retraceable or retrievable at any stage and one which is in touch with 'underlying order, a system of deep and simple systematic connections', which, 'if only they could be perceived to their fullest extent, would serve to explain all things'.[1]

In the context of British art Mary Kelly's *Post-Partum Document* is an example of precisely this attitude. The *Document,* started in 1974 and completed in 1979, assumed a research method which took its theoretical parameters from Marx, Freud and Lacan. The relationship between mother and child, after the point of physical separation at birth, was given a material and aesthetic parallel in the developing form of the *Document* itself. By adopting a critical method to treat the most intimate of social exchanges, Kelly placed her experience in the objective realm of social anthropology as opposed to personal anecdote.

Crucial to this kind of art is the forcing of the distinction between 'seeing' and 'reading'. To 'see' is to apprehend the thing itself; to 'read', on the other hand, is to reach beyond its physical attributes – it establishes a relationship with that 'underlying order'. From Giorgione to Picasso and beyond, all art has required of the viewer both levels of assimilation, reading as well as seeing. However, for artists up to the middle of the nineteenth century, the idea of reading was closely attached to representation and therefore focused on the interpretation of iconography. With Impressionism all this changed. An alliance was forged between scientific method and artistic vision which signalled a new concept of visual language. Thenceforth the modern artist would speak no more of 'pictorial language'. He or she might speak of 'picture' in certain prescribed circumstances, or indeed of 'language', but never in the same breath.

The crucial modernist separation had been made – which not only changed the perception of artists in relation to their task, but also changed the role of the viewer. It was no longer possible to play the passive spectator; the comfortable cocoon of illusionism had been dismantled. From then on, every image was virgin territory – a new world with its own language, a code to be cracked. And every new language was to require of the respondent a purposeful act of imaginative construction. It is almost the definitive characteristic of the modern work of art that it seeks to place the viewer alongside the artist in this critical position – in or astride the gap between 'seeing' and 'reading', knowingly constructing the art object and at the same time reconstructing the self as a responding, participating subject. With the emphasis placed on the generation of language or languages in opposition to the traditional trappings of mimesis, the modern artist is continuously in a critical relationship to his or her means of expression: the condition of modern art is shown to be reflexive.

Many individual artists have made this reflexive process the central theme of their work. For them, to bring art so firmly within the domain of language is to make it clearly part of culture and distinct from nature. Nevertheless, the objects of art enter the natural world. They can therefore employ something of its behavioural rhetoric – the language of gesture, for instance – and can parallel some of its processes of operation – lying, stacking, leaning, etc. Beyond this, art remains essentially relational and abstract.

The taut – the straightening and stretching, sometimes arcing – lines in the sculpture of Anthony Caro, are redolent with bodily presence, which is their point of contact with the natural world. Yet they are more than frozen gestures clinging stubbornly to reality. Through Caro's attention to the demands of sculptural language, one is brought to that point – both historical and experiential – where the need for language is first understood.

The same process is at work in the less formal sculptures of Richard Long. For Long, the setting is nature; the action is the imposition of a line or circle, made or walked. The effect is to confront nature with the 'indifference' of geometry, represented by the 'cruel' act of drawing. The harshness of his assault on the natural world is always well disguised; cloaked in ironic attentiveness, he rehearses the rituals of barely cultured man but he does so from the high ground of sophisticated contemporary culture. Lines, circles, marks of hands are the evidence of human presence, and their ordering is the first sign of human culture – primal language.

In the language of film the camera's eye, its gaze, is perhaps the nearest equivalent to the kind of drawing which Long undertakes in his walking pieces. The camera also traces a passage through reality, caressing everything in its visual field. The lens is intentionally focused and records the path of its intention. In so doing it establishes the interface between the medium of film and its subject. Paul Bush's film *The cow's drama* is exemplary in this respect. It is all about looking: the camera's indifferent eye watches farmer and cow, cow and calf locked together in the recurring drama of their daily round. Bush's involvement is undoubtedly subjective; his method of observation is objective. The result is the creation of an ironic distance which is interposed not simply between the film-maker and his subject but between the audience and the film as an object of the audience's attention. In the end, language supersedes narrative.

This form of drawing, then, is the direct trace connecting action and thought. At the simplest level drawing is the making of a mark, but it can function as schema, emblem and inscription, and this is clearly shown in Long's later 'word drawings'. In *Three Moors: Three Circles*, for instance, the contradictory schema of the piece is set, on the one hand, by the placing of the title two-thirds of the way down the page, which suggests an elevation – the basic landscape division between earth and sky – and, on the other, by the concentric circles, which are seen as plan. We are therefore presented with a problem of reading, and are offered no easy solution. Instead, we are left to slip sideways into the emblematic – seeing the page as a set of simple signs: sun; sky; horizon; earth. Thence we return the word to its prime function of naming, placing and describing – we see the page as inscription. His actions, walking the circles and walking the line, are constructions in language, part of the topology of mind.

In the wall drawings and relief constructions of Michael Craig-Martin and the sculptures of Tony Cragg we can see a similar breaking down of emblem to reveal more intricate levels of reading. In Craig-Martin's work this is in part a product of scale. Drawings are expanded to a size at which the conventions that give the image its coherence start to function in an almost maverick fashion. Straight lines bend and twist; familiar objects distort and dislocate; the drawing is transformed into a network of nodal points, out of which sense has to be continually fought for and remade. In the reliefs this is carried a stage further. Through the intervention of the third dimension the schematic character of the line breaks down. *Sharp practice* – first of all an emblem, replete with powerful associations – is coolly and deliberately 'atomized' by the planal structure: language is robbed of its purpose and made the object of style. In this respect the works have a disarmingly seductive appearance. But there is also a hidden and more disturbing side to them – the emblem itself is made out to be little more than an accident of language; one of those occasional illusions of 'sense' which language throws up.

This Borgesian double bind is an important element in Cragg's work also. He starts with a common-or-garden image, which he remakes using a collection of found bits and pieces, coded according to shape, scale, character and material. All the elements are given equal weight; Cragg allows no formal or structural hierarchies in his work. Nor is there any attempt at crafting; when more than simple placing is needed he resorts to do-it-yourself engineering. His philosophy of making might be said to be that of least possible interference. In fact Cragg is holding the balance between two quite distinct orders of language: the grammatical and the lexical – the former concerned with making sense and the latter simply with the listing of parts. Once emblem is set aside, the sculpture is a kit of parts for us to make of what we will. We are faced with Borges's 'labyrinth': we become searchers after accidental truths.[2]

However, Cragg's sculptures are not an arbitrary scattering; more a painterly, 'restless accumulation' of objects across a constructed grid. These are qualities which the modern sculptor shares with more formally concerned performance artists. For example, Anthony Howell in his early work with the Theatre of Mistakes always worked with a strong sense of 'plan'. Plan provided a fixed order against which he could pitch time-based kinetic action – the movements of his performers. With the pace set by counting, an accumulation of errors led to chance events occurring out of overlapping cycles of action, thus generating a concatenation of chance and order. In the more recent solo pieces the ordering devices are less apparent, more hidden by the sequence of 'things to be done'. But the feeling of a submerged order at odds with human intentions, actions and desires remains, and it is this that compels our attention since it offers a possible level at which things might actually make sense. As always the ghost in the machine is – paradoxically – the human presence.

Howell allows himself no solace in abstractions: he must be seen to act in the real world. At first sight this appears to be the point at which he, although working with similar conceptual concerns, would seem to part company with a constructivist, non-figurative artist like Kenneth Martin. In Martin's work the numerical system which dictates the overall form of the work is sacrosanct. It is converted into a consistent visual language by using multiples of a fixed linear unit. Martin, however, retains the essential aesthetic freedom of when and how to activate his system. Both coherent choice and intuitive judgment are contained within an abstract network of formal relationships, and language is realized as concrete order.

Artists like Susan Hiller and Joel Fisher view language from a very different perspective.

While Martin sees language as an all-embracing 'deep and simple system of connections', Hiller and Fisher return us to the view of language implied in the work of Long, Cragg and Craig-Martin — an unknowable domain which is continually throwing up the illusions of sense and order, an effective 'veil' beyond which we can never quite see. Susan Hiller's recent work focuses our attention on precisely this veil, on to which she 'projects' the most primitive forms of utterance, signs and sounds, which are like the written and oral fragments of a language for which we no longer have the rules. She invites us, through the projection of our own sophisticated grammar and syntax, to search for the traces of a coherent structure which will offer us the opportunity of making sense. But her invitation is an invitation to transgress, to invade the site of language beyond the veil, which we can never actually occupy. The ironic analogy which Hiller invites is that of being transported beyond the veil of death to the world of spirit; we are to pass over temporarily to the other side, there to discover a different notion of sense, a new *raison d'être*. At the same time we are left no alternative but to see that this is an illusion.

For Joel Fisher the act of paper making is a similar kind of metaphysical conundrum. Each new sheet of paper becomes 'a barrier, a gate: an image of each and, simultaneously, a space in which a new universe (or an image of an old one) can find a base'.[3] It is a metaphor for the 'veil', requiring a state of rapt attention to yield up an image, which is then drawn on to its surface. But in reality the image is called forth by Fisher's imagination — it is *his* projection, identified and articulated by his drawing, thus returned to the surface of language. He emphasizes this turning away from the abstract by reinterpreting the drawn image as a fully rounded sculptural object. Cast in bronze, carved in wood or stone, it enters the natural world. It is a transitional object between the two domains of language.

JON THOMPSON

NOTES

1 Extract from a definition of science in C. G. Hempel, *Recent Problems of Induction — in Mind and Cosmos*, University of Pittsburgh Press, Pittsburgh, 1966.

2 Jorge Luis Borges, 'The Library of Babel', *Labyrinths*, Penguin, Harmondsworth, 1970.

3 Joel Fisher, 'Sitting on the Gate', in *Joel Fisher*, catalogue of an exhibition, Kunstmuseum Luzern, 1984.

KENNETH MARTIN
CHANCE ORDER CHANGE 27,
HISTORY PAINTING
1983
oil on canvas
91.4 x 116.5 cm

ANTHONY CARO
BOMBAZINE
1980-2
brass and bronze, cast and welded
87.6 x 92.7 x 63.5 cm

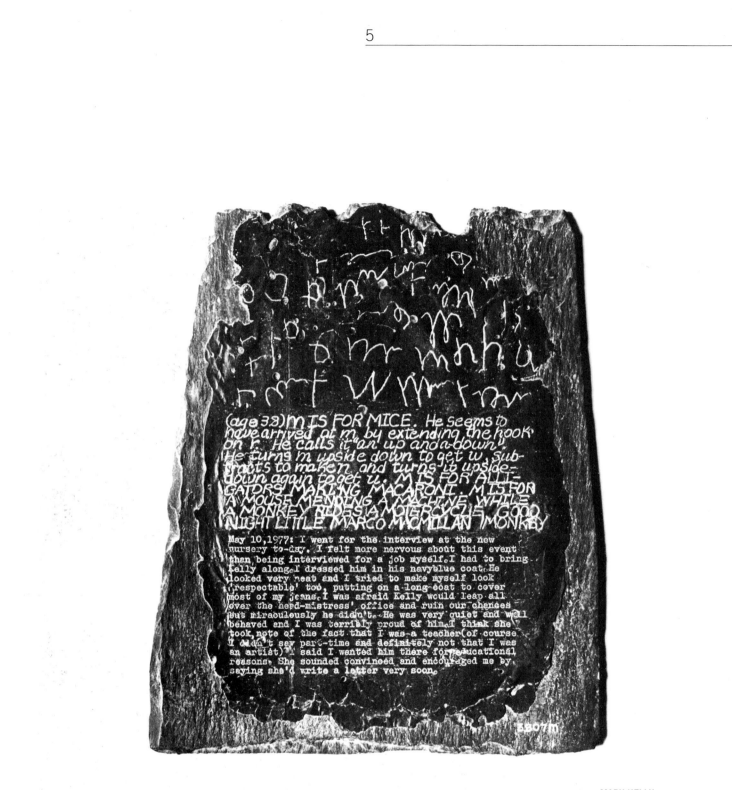

MARY KELLY
POST-PARTUM DOCUMENT
DOCUMENTATION VI
PRE-WRITING ALPHABET,
EXERQUE AND DIARY
1979
resin and slate
15 units 20.3 x 25.4 cm

PAUL BUSH
from THE COW'S DRAMA
1983
16mm film; 38 minutes
black and white
magnetic sound

ANTHONY HOWELL
TABLE MOVE II
1983
Lyons International Symposium
of Performance Art

RICHARD LONG
THREE MOORS THREE CIRCLES
1982
printed work
103 x 153 cm

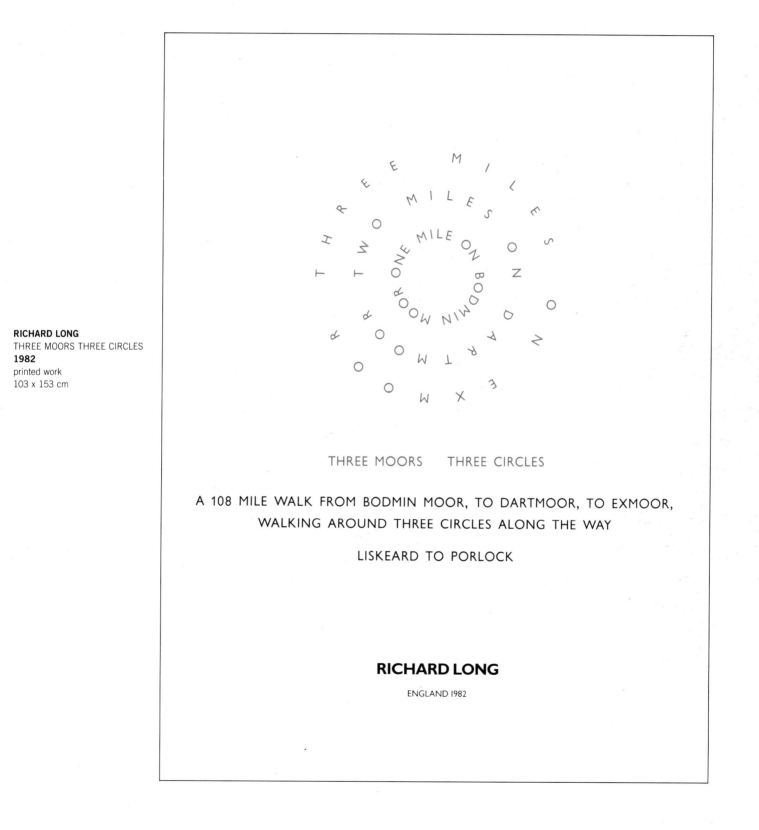

THREE MOORS   THREE CIRCLES

A 108 MILE WALK FROM BODMIN MOOR, TO DARTMOOR, TO EXMOOR,
WALKING AROUND THREE CIRCLES ALONG THE WAY

LISKEARD TO PORLOCK

RICHARD LONG

ENGLAND 1982

TONY CRAGG
OPENING SPIRAL
1982
mixed media -- found objects
152 x 408 x 152 cm

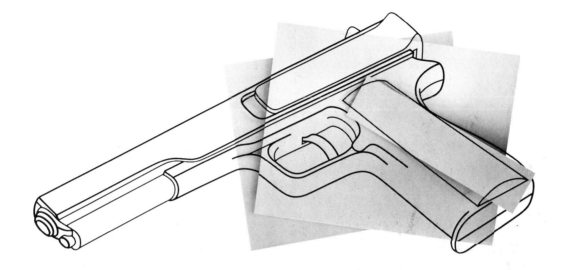

MICHAEL CRAIG-MARTIN
SHARP PRACTICE
1984
oil on aluminium panels with
painted steel lines
91.4 x 213.4 x 25.4 cm approx.

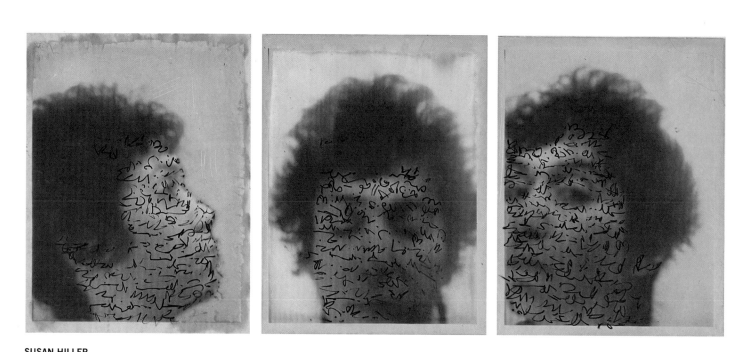

SUSAN HILLER
MIDNIGHT, BAKER STREET
1983
set of 3 C-type photographs,
enlarged from hand-coloured
automatic photographs
each 71 x 51 cm

JOEL FISHER
PAPABILUS
1982-4
bronze
58 x 66 x 48 cm

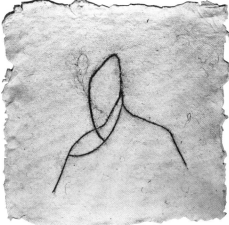

PRESENTING REALITY

Art is not a copy of the real world. One of the damn things is enough. (attributed to Virginia Woolf)[1]

Can we describe a photograph as a 'representation'? If we can, do we mean the same thing as when we apply the term to painting? At first sight this looks like one of those numbing technical questions on which philosophers and aestheticians sharpen their wits – of no practical interest either to artists or to the public at large. Yet it is an issue raised by the work of many artists in the post-Conceptual period. For such artists the preferred term would seem to be 'presentation' – where a painting 'represents', a photograph 'presents'. This nice distinction is founded upon different degrees of mediation and dissimilar processes of transformation. 'Presentation' demands a quite new explanation of the relationship of the artist to the imaging process, and a different status for the image itself in relation to its source in the real world.

The concept of representation (re-presenting) is inseparable from the history of painting. The painter inevitably mediates between the 'subject' and the image. The search is always for a coherence of style and language which will adequately represent the subject. Even in the most mimetic of painterly styles – in trompe l'oeil painting, for instance, where the object of the exercise is to deceive the eye, or in photo-realism, which seeks to imitate the surface characteristic of the photograph – the painter's intervention can never be lost altogether. Viewed from a certain distance the image breaks down into 'language' – one might even say into hand-writing – into marks and accumulations of marks, into shapes and colours. Painting, then, is perhaps best described as the 're-presenting' of a subject in painterly language. Such a description defines painting as an act of material transformation and the painter's task as the constructing of an intelligible symbolic order.

The photographer may determine, to a very considerable extent, the configuration of the subject, but he or she cannot intervene between lens and film. The camera receives the image ready-made. Its initial impression rules all, down to the last speck of grain, and the closest possible scrutiny reveals no other linguistic order. Such coherence as it possesses subsists in this one simple fact. This raises the question of whether the photographic imprint can be said to be a language, and it is an intriguing one. In painting, the moment at which illusion and allusion give way in favour of the material attributes of the paint as language is always clear. In the case of photography, there is no such moment. The ghost of its origin in reality is indelible. The photograph refuses to surrender its role as a bearer of information. In short it always functions as a presentiment of the real. On this basis alone, it is reasonable to argue that the photograph is indeed more of a 'presentation' than a 'representation'. Accidents of light shape the image. There is no handwriting. We might almost describe the photograph as a back-projection which presents itself as integral to the 'screen's' surface.

The unity between image and vehicle has made photography of particular interest to artists wishing to set aside the traditional view of imaging as 're-presentation'. The issue was first aired by the Minimalists, artists like Don Judd, Sol le Witt and Robert Morris. Their attack was directed at what they chose to call 'expressionism' – a catch-all critical term which threatened the end of referential language and ultimately the demise of representational art. 'Expressionism' was to be replaced by what Don Judd called an art of 'specific objects'. The 'minimal' object carried neither references nor allusions; it stubbornly refused to represent. Its sole purpose was to elicit a clear range of perceptual responses from the spectator. It was this aspect of Minimalism which caused it to be dubbed 'theatrical'.

Minimalism's theatricality insisted upon a 'presentational' rather than a representational mode of address. Language became synonymous with material structure. Subject and object were made one, in an airless and unyielding unity. It was this which provided the springboard for the critical task of Conceptual Art – which paved the way for the art object to be dispensed with altogether. Art could indeed be reduced to verbal propositions and/or statements, if language could be shown to be no more than a form of presentation.

Minimalism in its strictest form, never really took a hold in Britain. Nevertheless the presentational theory on which it was based achieved widespread acceptance amongst young British artists. It manifested itself in peculiarly British ways, most of which emphasized its tendency towards theatricality. In general it resulted in a migration of artists away from the traditional disciplines of painting and sculpture and into performance art, photography and the kinetic media. They were seeking linguistic anonymity; wishing to present the 'subject' as a *fait accompli* rather than a construction in language. Whatever the medium adopted, the intention was to present the mute drama of image not as a thing to be looked at, but as the surface of the 'screen' upon which reality is projected.

Among the artists who chose photography, John Hilliard's work provides the purest example of this strategy of presentation. For him, all is prescribed by the behaviour of the camera; the image reveals the camera's role as well as being a record of the subject. Hilliard takes an inordinate amount of care in siting and setting up the *mise-en-scène*, which must be capable of exploiting the camera's capacity to change its focal depth from foreground to background, and must also offer opportunity for the partial retention or dissolving of the image when the camera moves. The scene is 'scripted' for cameraman and model. Time-based action within a fixed setting determines the eventual form of the image. An engagement with one of Hilliard's photographs requires a considerable amount of detective work. We have to reconstruct two distinct but overlapping orbits of action, one of which is the trace of the movement of the subject, and the other – often incorporated within the image by the use of mirrors – the movement of the camera. We are forced then to realize the image as the trace of a real event.

Although the style of the imagery is very different, Boyd Webb also contrives highly elaborate sets, incorporating figures and objects. The finished photographs have the appearance of being matter-of-fact records of surreal tableaux, or even of wildly experimental window displays. They employ witty exaggerations and crushing visual puns, in ways which seem to poke fun at the material limitations and traditional concerns of sculpture – but they also demand scrutiny at a deeper level. The images are built throughout on metaphor: carpet, its pile uppermost, becomes grass, sea, even the face of the moon; turned over it is rock or an elephant's skin; paper is turned into sky or breaking waves; cardboard into the side of an ocean-going liner and polystyrene foam into clouds or virgin snowfields. The inhabitants of these makeshift worlds have tasks to perform which expose his depiction of the elements as fiction, and by so doing continually refer us back to the artifice of the scene as a whole. Boyd Webb's absurd theatre is recorded with impartiality by the eye of the camera; the image, so carefully contrived, appears as little more than an accident of its romance with reality.

Much contemporary work in film and video uses techniques which highlight the artificiality of the medium. Working from uncut footage to arrive at the finished product, the film-maker, like the painter, is inevitably caught up in the making of language, including the degree to which language is made apparent to the viewer. In the commercial worlds of cinema and television, devices like cutting and cropping are used to construct a 'seamless', smooth-flowing narrative, or to emphasize the dramatic structure. In any event the devices are not to be noticed. In 'art' film and video the reverse is often true; these same devices are used to bring attention to the language of the medium itself. In Sandra Goldbacher's work, staccato cutting and the montage and overlaying of scratch material taken from old Hollywood films are used to show how the camera stereotypes and fetishizes the objects of its gaze. Both Goldbacher and Mick Hartney are in different ways concerned to contrast the image as a faithful trace of reality with it in its most transformed and mediated state. In Goldbacher's work this is done by introducing into the shifting mirage of second-hand material instances of live action. In Hartney's work the opposite strategy is adopted. He inserts highly coloured polarized images to work against the realism implied by the cool, documentary style of his camera work.

While the kinetic media can shift emphasis easily between the domain of language and an illusion of reality, the same flexibility is not available to the painter. The painter cannot elude the material limitations of the painting format. It is this problem that Gerard Hemsworth addresses in his paintings. Hemsworth uses photography as a source, not of imagery as such – he photographs his own subjects – but for the appearance that it gives to things, something he seeks to retain in the painted form. The images themselves tread the line between pathos and bathos, between high drama and high comedy. They exploit incongruous relationships and extreme contradictions of scale. An important aspect of the work is clearly that the significance of the total image should remain obscure and therefore a matter for speculation. In contrast to the way he treats the images, the treatment of the painting overall is severely formal. The integrity of the picture surface is sacrosanct and the individual 'photographic' fragments adhere to it like great big transfers. Three distinct domains of experience emerge: the perceptual – the apprehension of things as things; the aesthetic – the constructing of the image as language; and the interpretive – the way we give meaning to what we see. In an integral form, Hemsworth demonstrates precisely those divisions which John Smith addresses as in his recent film *Shepherd's Delight*. Smith uses the illustrated lecture in order to parody semiological analyses and to satirize the role of the semiologist.[2] He looks to the world of packaging and advertising for his examples, and these are treated by his lecturer to an analysis which raises the concept of 'deep structure' to the heights of absurdity. Hidden behind the welter of pseudo-analysis is a world of ordinary people with ordinary concerns. Through the advertisers' guiles and, in a different way, by the constructs of theoreticians, they are presented to themselves as quite other than what they are – as unwitting victims of perceptual tricks, incapable of interpreting the world in which they live. In his humorous way Smith wishes to show that they are not so easily bamboozled by the manipulation of language.

Ray Smith, by comparison, finds his solution by enthusiastically embracing the artifice of visual language. He incorporates photographic material of all kinds with television images, children's drawings and Disney cartoons to create an almost childlike fantasy world, which he presents with the extravagant theatricality of pantomime. Like pantomime, it treats of good and evil but in an unfailingly winsome way. Like Goldbacher, he uses media imagery to underline its separateness from reality – to show that the representation can be more real than its subject. Not surprisingly, he often paints theatre pictures. It is the place where fantasy can come alive, where cartoon characters can strut and posture before a packed auditorium, rendered as a black-and-white photograph, where they can cast real shadows on an illusory world. In the seaside illumination pictures, this same theme is carried a stage further; figures and objects drawn in light are made so insistent that the real world disappears altogether, is lost in darkness. Smith's preoccupation with media imagery then, is heavily ironic; it is his way of dealing with reality without appearing to look it in the eye.

The irony in Marc Chaimowicz's work is of a very different order. He too gives full scope to artifice, but in his case it is cast in a unifying style. Chaimowicz presents us with the consistent elegance of a beautifully crafted and highly aesthetic model world, which is placed within the real world. It is intended that we should see through it to the arbitrary and accidental character of the common or garden. We are made accomplices in Chaimowicz's autobiographical strategy of narcissistic mirroring, seeing both realities and belonging to neither. Unlike Ray Smith who refuses to personalize fantasy, preferring to see it as a product of culture, Chaimowicz ties fantasy to his artistic persona, thus projecting himself as an ironic fiction.

This strategy of self-presentation, which has its origin in performance art, is also shared by Helen Chadwick and Gilbert & George. Chadwick explores the relationship between geometry – as a representation of absolute beauty and harmony – and lived and living reality, her own body. She presents geometry by a series of solids, overlaid with photographic images of herself. The images are cast over the solids like transparent veils, leaving the material presence of the forms intact. The effect is a curious metaphysical reversal in which abstract form is made more concrete than reality. Reality has made but a fugitive impression, and the whole stands as a metaphor for the transience of life.

The most extreme example of the presentation of the persona of the artist as ironic fiction is to be found in the work of Gilbert & George. It is made doubly ironic by the fact that they are two and not one. In terms of the image they retain distinct personalities, but in terms of the content of the work they would seem to think as one mind. Nor are we granted insight into exactly how that mind is constituted. Is it the common denominator of two minds or an agreed fiction, which leaves them both free to think their own thoughts? The question is posed, and left deliberately unanswered by all that they do. It is what gives the work its aggressive edge, more so even than their subject matter – it is what causes our acute unease. They present an impenetrable façade, decorated with a parade of grotesqueries springing from the darker side of the human condition; a kind of medieval drama in which they appear as Mephisto-phelian proponents of self-indulgence, oppression and corruption. Once again the photo-graphic image is used as a synonym for reality, to reflect rather than to represent; it is documentary evidence that things are the way they appear to be. The strategy is that of mirroring; the enigmatic oneness that is Gilbert & George reflects all that is behind us, as we stand and look, and nothing of what is beyond the mirror. We are made uncomfortably a part of that 'real' world which is the subject of their ironic gaze. We stand accused of complicity in its most brutish and negative utterances and actions.

JON THOMPSON

NOTES

1 Nelson Goodman, *Languages of Art*, Hackett, Indiana-polis, 1976.

2 Semiology: a term borrowed from medicine – in which discipline it means the reading of symptoms – to in-augurate the modern 'science' of signs and symbols. This science treats all systems of signs and symbols, including written language, as indicative ('symptomatic') of a significant deep structure or order.

JOHN HILLIARD
MASQUERADE
1982
cibachromes on aluminium
80 x 200 cm

JOHN SMITH
from SHEPHERD'S DELIGHT
1980-4
16 mm film: 36 minutes,
colour, sound

MICK HARTNEY
from DICKLER'S WHAMMY –
A FICTION
1982-3
colour videotape: 17 minutes,
stereo sound

GILBERT & GEORGE
BLOODED
1983
photo-piece
302.5 x 252.5 cm

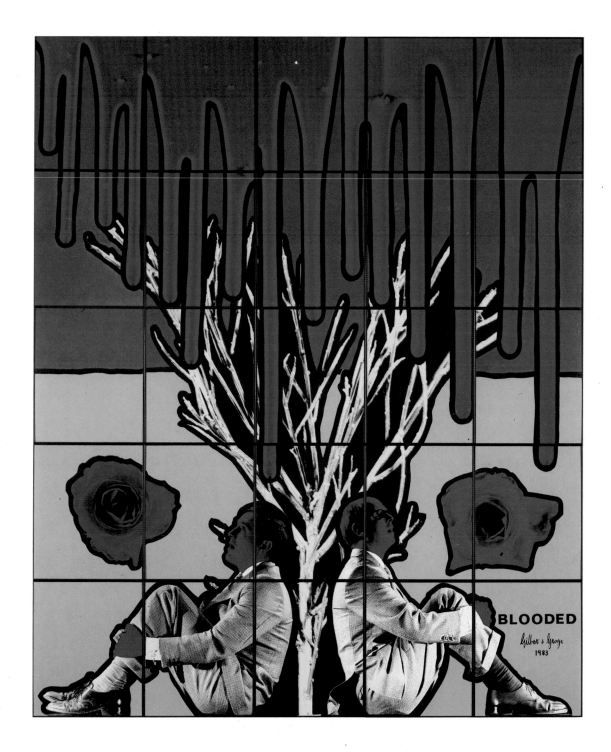

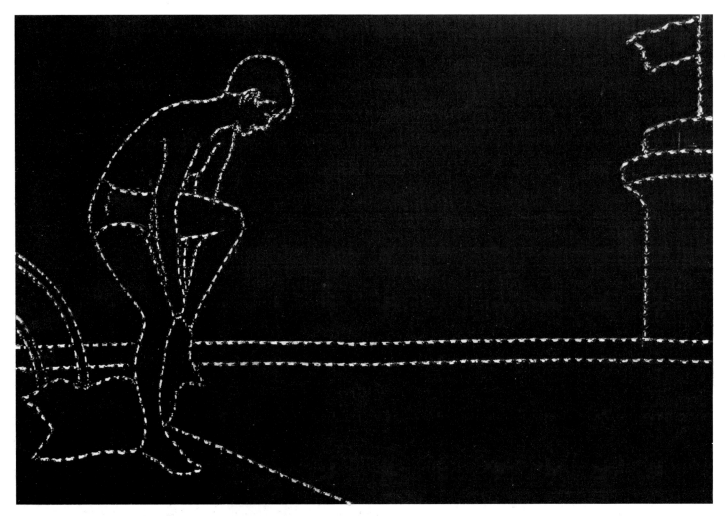

RAY SMITH
THE YOUNG BATHER
1982
acrylic on canvas
152.4 x 213.4 cm

HELEN CHADWICK
EGO GEOMETRIA SUM IX:
HIGH SCHOOL – AGE 13
1983
plywood and photographic emulsion
70 x 70 x 70 cm

GERARD HEMSWORTH
DELUGE
1983
acrylic on canvas
244 x 153 cm

BOYD WEBB
NOURISH
1984
unique colour photograph
151 x 121 cm

SANDRA GOLDBACHER
from POLKA DOTS
AND MOONBEAMS
1983
colour videotape
13½ minutes

MARC CHAIMOWICZ
GENEVA DIPTYCH, LEANING . . .
WITH CHORUS GIRLS AND
SENTINELS
WINTER 1984
2 glass panels, 5 wood panels,
photographs, oil medium,
gloss paint
180 x 370 cm approx.
(not in exhibition)

RETRIEVING THE IMAGE

Who is a painter, after all? Man is an image-maker and painting is image-making. The abstract painters – what are they telling us? That this is absolute? Well, all right, so is this beer glass. But what else is man? (Philip Guston)[1]

With those words the American painter Philip Guston spoke aloud the thoughts and feelings that many artists were beginning to formulate in the seventies. Guston, who was born in 1913, worked on the Works Progress Administration mural projects in the thirties and after the war he became associated with the New York school of Abstract Expressionists. In the late sixties he became dissatisfied with the limitations of Abstraction and started to paint 'common objects, things rooted in the visible world'. Those late monumental works, painted between 1970 and his death in 1980, were met with uncertainty and suspicion when first shown in New York, where for many in the art world his return to the painting of real objects was an act of betrayal. For others, his powerful images of a personal and universal hell, simultaneously grotesque and serious, underlined the need for an art which could take on more, an art which could deal with the broader issues of the human condition. The implications of Guston's last paintings and his seminal (though much misunderstood) position in relation to the New Art have been immensely important in helping to open the door on to the present hectic preoccupation with the image.

John Berger commented that 'It is not – and never has been – a question of all abstract art being fundamentally opposed to figurative art', and of course, Guston wasn't the first artist to turn back from Abstraction to representation.[2] It is also true that many who have done so, have returned to a safe and well-trodden path, adopting a negative and self-righteous stance against all forms of Modernism. Guston's aim was to increase the range and diversity of modern painting, not to fall back into a defunct traditionalism. There are distinct connections and parallels between abstract and figurative tendencies throughout the modern era – only after 1945 did the insistence on absolute faithfulness to one or the other become the accepted dogma. The impact of Abstract Expressionism in particular, with its emphasis on painterly gesture, has had a pronounced influence on figurative painting, especially on a number of the younger 'imagists'. Indeed, many notable figurative artists have gone through an abstract phase. John Walker has travelled from the Goya-inspired figuration of his student years, via a post-Cubist abstraction of structures and shapes, to an imagery which now stops just short of Abstraction. Ken Kiff embraced formal Abstraction in his early days and John Bellany was influenced when young by the magical improvisations of Alan Davie. The foolish practice of combining elements from both languages to concoct a pseudo-modern style does not concern us here; what does, is the problematic and complex task of infusing a language with new vigour.

Both Francis Bacon and David Hockney have offered solutions to this problem – solutions which differ immensely in style and content from those of the new generation of imagists. Although Bacon, who has remained a major painter of images since the end of the forties, equates Abstraction with decoration, his distaste for illustrational or story-telling figuration in its simplest manifestation has led to his use of sources from modern design and photography. Hockney has also specialized in the use of photography as information for his paintings. He is fascinated by the flow of visual information which inundates contemporary life and by the riches of twentieth-century art. His ideal is to make the diversity of Modernism into a synthesis.

'I am an eclectic artist. I feel that there's nothing stopping me now from painting almost anything, even just some stripes if I want, it can all fit in with a view. I feel that some older figurative painters aren't aware of any recent art history at all. Their art doesn't show it; there's no reference to the great complexity of the last 50 years.'[3] Hockney's own brand of eclecticism has taken in the world of Parisian modernity during the twenties and thirties – Picasso, Matisse and Dufy. With the arrival of the new European Painting, the 'Pseudo-Expressionists', the 'Trans Avant-Garde', the 'Neue Wilden' (all already labelled), and with the emergence of a new figuration in Britain, the ideas surrounding 'post-Modernist' eclecticism have taken on different meanings and directions.

The sophisticated urbanity peculiar to the paintings of Bacon and Hockney, Kitaj's painting of ideas, indeed any kind of contemporary realism, whether photographic in origin or inspired by the stereotyped images of the mass media so uncritically celebrated by the Pop artists of the sixties, seem remote from the new forms of symbolic content which the artists showing here have developed. Only Bacon's alienated human image, his despairing view of life, finds echoes in the claustrophobic and disturbing imagery of John Bellany, Philip Nicol and Jayne Parker. As Pop Art was conceived out of a counter-movement to two decades of Abstract domination, the new imagery has emerged as a reaction to a dying and weary formalism. For younger artists such as Tony Bevan, Philip Nicol and Andrew Walker, who have worked their way through the influences of American Abstraction and Conceptual Art, a theoretical advance towards the image takes into account a dialogue with both Abstraction and Conceptual Art. This conversion to imagery after the reductivist and fundamentalist obsessions of the previous generation may have come as a surprise, but those so-called 'new' concerns of representation and meaning allied to a language of figuration have always been around.

The main strands of this movement in Britain are very different from those at present dominating Western Europe and America. The themes of history and politics which have so gripped German artists, the nostalgia and pastiche which involves Italian artists, and the concentration of the New York 'image scavengers' on the mass media are far removed from the intentions of British artists. There are no real schools of imagists here, although some have occasionally taught together in art schools. There are few coherent groups, if any, meeting regularly to develop aesthetic plans or manifestoes. The British scene comprises artists from vastly different backgrounds where their individual aims and skills have grown in comparative isolation from each other. The 'New Image' work currently sweeping through the galleries is largely alien to them. Unlike the fashionable manufactured 'heroes' and 'heroines' of the international art scene, many British figurative artists have developed their styles and ideas in opposition to the rules of the art game. Being treated as misfits over the years has helped rather than hindered, and their stature and maturity when compared to the recent whizz kids are strikingly obvious. The creation of a new language is not the overriding ambition of artists such as John Bellany, Ken Kiff, Paula Rego or John Walker – it is instead the expression of feeling harnessed to an individual vision and experience of the world. This vision is certainly 'expressionist' in nature but theirs is an expressionism which is not confined to a mere stylistic school, but is, as Herbert Read observed, 'one of the basic modes of perceiving and representing the world around us'.[4] After the void which characterized the art of the sixties and seventies these artists present to us an emotional authenticity and a directness of expression which communicates with great immediacy. Their search for the memorable image is undertaken with an instinctive and urgent need.

A romantic quest to understand the world around them, and humanity's role in it, pervades the work of the artists in this section. Though, at times, a confusion of symbols and private images makes interpretation difficult, the struggle of those artists to come to terms with the mystery of existence has thrown up a remarkable variety of riches. The myths invoked are not those of ancient history, but originate from a deeply felt personal involvement with themes and subjects over a long period – Kiff's fables drawing on primal and archetypal situations; Bellany's allegorical scenes of the North Sea, its fisherfolk and their fate; Rego's view of the human comedy, satirically attributing human behaviour to animals, exposes folly and stupidity. Images of life and death, of love and sex, of pain and suffering, are rarely far from the surface as a troubled examination of the human condition engages all those artists, no matter how dissimilar their vision or ultimate goal. Not all of the imagists work in an overtly subjective manner – Tony Bevan's emblematic figures, Andrew Walker's decorative arcadian land-scapes and Antony Gormley's sculptures of the human body all project an identity which owes little to Expressionism. The simplification and stillness of Gormley's sculpture, his use of the figure as a metaphor for various inner states, his restrained evocation of spirituality, contrast vividly with the tormented and dramatic visions which crowd the galleries, distorting our age's right to reclaim the image.

The neo-Romantic tendencies which have prevailed in recent art seem far removed from contemporary actuality; the new imagery more often than not suggests an adaptation of old imagery, harking back to the 'decadent' world of certain late nineteenth-century movements rather than forward towards the twenty-first century. Today's imagery with its emphasis and dependence on symbols and emblems suggests an escape, a departure from the modern world and from the aims of earlier modern figurative masters – even Munch, Kirchner and the Brücke group seem much more of our century than the 'primitives' of the eighties. This return to a world of myth and fantasy which so distinguishes the imagery of our day from the imagery of the previous two decades has been interpreted as a morbid retreat from rational thought. The reinstatement of figuration is also criticized as a symptom of increasing political oppres-sion and passivity in the Western world. Another view, however, suggests that the creation of a mythical and symbolic world is needed to counteract the potential nightmare that technology has become and reflects an awareness that man is now more fully equipped than at any previous time to completely destroy himself. Only in this sense have the purveyors of myth sought to come to terms with their own times.

In a lecture given in 1938 the German painter Max Beckmann said: 'The elimination of the human component from artistic representation is the cause of the vacuum which makes us all suffer in varying degrees. . . . Human sympathy and understanding must be reinstated.'[5] This year is the centenary of his birth and his formidable influence hovers uncomfortably over the art of our period. Today Beckmann is recognized as one of the great masters of the Modern Movement. How different things are from the sixties when his large retrospective exhibition at the Tate Gallery (1965) went largely ignored (the so-called 'central' tradition of Modernism was then moving in a different direction). Beckmann's paintings, full of literary and mythological references seem to have become a model for much of today's imagery; his 'transcendental objectivity' and striving towards a new spiritual climate has echoed throughout the artistic landscape of the eighties. What real significance does his art have in relation to present-day events?

As each historical period presents some form of unity in thought and style, Beckmann, like Gustav Mahler (who was also ignored for many years), can be seen as a prophetic figure whose overwhelming sense of humanity centres on a vision of spirituality, rising above the abyss of twentieth-century materialism. His predilection for catastrophic subject matter, his concern for 'the great orchestra of humanity' and his desire to paint for mankind 'a picture of their fate' have yet to find real parallels in current artistic activity but artists no longer deny those necessary pursuits.

The main achievement of all the artists represented here, from Bellany to Willing, has been to create an imaginary world which can make available to others the thoughts and feelings of their inner world. An art of dreams and fantasy illuminating another reality may well suggest an adoption of mystical and quasi-religious beliefs in an irrational withdrawal from contemporary issues and problems. Alternatively, it can be hailed as an attempt to supply the imagery for a modern mythology, arising from a profound understanding of the fundamental pattern of the human spirit. Now that modern art has convincingly rediscovered the human image, now that artists are again representing reality in an effort to penetrate 'the mystery of being', art must communicate its sense of purpose and meaning if it is to retain a central function in our lives and reach an audience anxiously awaiting an art of intensity.

ALEXANDER MOFFAT

NOTES

1 Quoted in Dore Ashton, *Yes, but . . . A Critical Study of Philip Guston.* Viking Press, New York, 1976.

2 John Berger, 'The difficulty of being an artist – the Biennale', in *Permanent Red.* Methuen, London, 1960.

3 *David Hockney by David Hockney,* ed. Nikos Stangos, Thames & Hudson, London, 1976.

4 Herbert Read, 'Expressionism and idealism', in *The Meaning of Art.* Revised edn, Penguin in association with Faber & Faber, Harmondsworth, 1959.

5 Max Beckmann, 'On my painting', a lecture given at the New Burlington Galleries, London, 21 July 1938, quoted in *Max Beckmann, catalogue of an exhibition at Marlborough Fine Art, London, November 1974.*

JOHN BELLANY
JANUS
1983
oil on canvas
172.7 x 122 cm

PAULA REGO
LA BOHÈME
1983
acrylic on paper
240 x 203 cm

JOHN WALKER
OCEANIA MY DILEMMA II
1983-4
oil on canvas
215.9 x 508 cm

VICTOR WILLING
PLACE WITH A RED THING
1980
oil on canvas
200 x 250 cm

KEN KIFF
THE FEMININE AS GENEROUS,
FRIGHTENING AND SERENE
1982-3
oil on canvas
160 x 129.5 cm

TONY BEVAN
BREAD AND COFFEE
1983
pigment and acrylic on canvas
184 x 162 cm

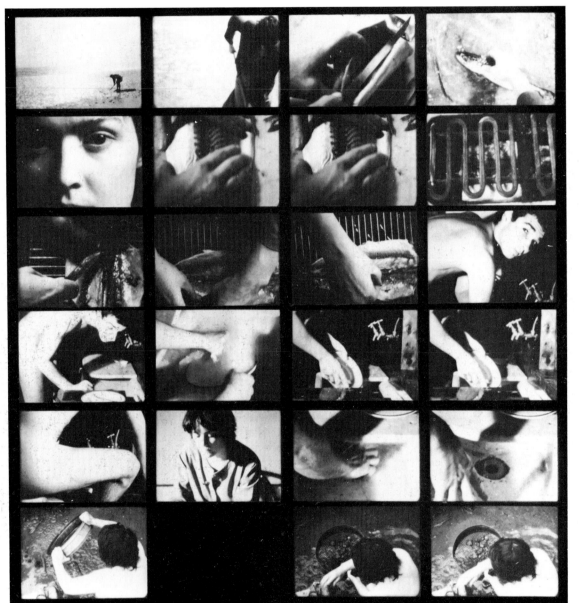

JAYNE PARKER
FROM 'I DISH'
1982
16 mm film, 16 minutes,
black and white,
magnetic sound

ANTONY GORMLEY
THREE CALLS: PASS,
CAST AND PLUMB
1983-4
lead, plaster, air
and fibreglass
pass: 190 x 56 x 95 cm
cast: 101 x 68 x 66 cm
plumb: 70 x 57 x 74 cm
(not in exhibition)

PHILIP NICOL
DOUBLE-TAKE
1982
acrylic on cotton duck
305 x 366 cm

ANDREW WALKER
ANGEL AND BLUE CAT
JUNE 1982
oil on canvas
114.3 x 91.4 cm

CATALOGUE

Catalogue Note

Where artists are represented by a gallery, this is given at the end of their biographical entry. When no gallery is given, artists can be contacted through the Arts Council, tel. no. 01 629 9495.

Sandra Goldbacher and Mick Hartney: videotapes available from London Video Arts, tel. no. 01 734 7410
Paul Bush and John Smith: films available from London Film Makers Co-op, tel. no. 01 586 4806
Jayne Parker: films available from Circles, tel. no. 01 981 6828.

ART & LANGUAGE
Founded 1967. Fifteen solo exhibitions since 1979 in Paris, Antwerp, Leeds, London, Eindhoven, Gent, Geneva, Middelburg, Toulon, Birmingham, Vienna and Los Angeles. Contributed to group exhibitions since 1979 in Paris, Glasgow, Gent, London, Tokyo, Vancouver, Kassel and Cologne. Most recent publication: *Art-Language*, Vol. 5 No. 2, March 1984.
Lisson Gallery, London

1
PAUL SIGNAC, LE PROFOND RÊVE D'AVENIR 1983
oil on canvas
305 x 488 cm
the artists, courtesy Lisson Gallery, London

KEVIN ATHERTON
Born Isle of Man 1950. Since 1982 produced television works in Amsterdam, 'Video Times' installation and publication in Birmingham and Cambridge, and sculpture installations for sites in London and the Garden Festival in Liverpool. Now working with Central Television, Birmingham, on a 30-minute television piece.

2
TELEVISION INTERVIEW 1984
video installation

TERRY ATKINSON
Born Thurnscoe, Yorkshire, 1939. Since 1979 produced papers on Realist Art, Modernism and the notion of the skill of drawing, among other articles and publications. One-person retrospective show at the

Whitechapel Art Gallery, London, which toured to Birmingham, Londonderry, Leeds and Eindhoven.

3
IDEOLOGICALLY BATTERED POSTCARD FROM TROTSKY IN COYOACAN TO STALIN IN MOSCOW, DATED 1938 1981–2
mixed media
269 x 201 cm
the artist
illustrated p. 63

4
POSTCARD FROM TROTSKY IN CONCENTRATION CAMP IN NOVA SCOTIA 1917, TO JOHN LOCKE IN SOMERSET 1690 1982
acrylic and hats on canvas
221 x 193 cm
the artist

FRANK AUERBACH
Born Berlin 1931. In 1979, one-man exhibition at Bernard Jacobson Gallery, New York, and in 1982 one-man exhibition at Marlborough Gallery Inc., New York. Advised on installation of 'Late Sickert' exhibition held at Hayward Gallery, London, 1981, and wrote the catalogue foreword.
Marlborough Fine Art (London) Ltd

5
EUSTON STEPS – STUDY 1980–1
oil on board
122 x 152.4 cm
Arts Council of Great Britain
illustrated p. 33

6
LARGE HEAD OF J.Y.M. 1981
oil on board
66 x 61 cm
Marlborough Fine Art (London) Ltd

7
HEAD OF CHARLOTTE PODRO 1982
oil on paper
76.2 x 57.2 cm
Marlborough Fine Art (London) Ltd

GILLIAN AYRES
Born London 1930. Since 1979 included in many mixed exhibitions and held two one-person exhibitions, in 1981 at the Museum of Modern Art, Oxford, which toured to Rochdale, Birmingham and Glasgow, and then in 1983 at the Serpentine Gallery, London, which also

toured. In 1982 awarded prize in the John Moores Liverpool Exhibition and elected an ARA.
Knoedler Kasmin Ltd.

8
A BELT OF STRAW AND IVY BUDS 1983
oil on canvas
310 x 167.6 cm
Tim and Alexandra Hilton
illustrated p. 35

9
BLACK MOUNTAINS 1983
oil on canvas
285 x 287 cm
Knoedler Kasmin Ltd

JO BAER/BRUCE ROBBINS
Baer – born Seattle, USA, 1929. Robbins – born London 1946. Worked together since 1978. Had eight joint exhibitions since 1980 in New York, Cologne, Dublin, London and Amsterdam. Lived in Ireland until summer 1982, when they moved to London.
Edward Totah Gallery, London

10
JO BAER
CLEAVING (APART/TOGETHER) 1979
oil on canvas
213.4 x 152.4 cm
the artist, courtesy Edward Totah Gallery, London
illustrated p. 50

11
BRUCE ROBBINS
THE SNATCHER (The collector of genitals) 1981
oil on canvas
243 x 183 cm
the artist, courtesy Edward Totah Gallery, London
illustrated p. 50

PETER BAILEY
Born near Wrexham, North Wales 1944. Had three one-person exhibitions since 1979, at the Festival Gallery, Bath; Coracle Press, London; and Oriel, Cardiff. Given an award by the Welsh Arts Council in 1979, and one from the Oppenheim-John Downes Memorial Trust in 1983.

12
DAPHNE AND APOLLO (an attempted rape) 1983
mixed media
diameter 203 x 11.4 cm
the artist

13
P.C.B. IN ISENHEIM AND BUTETOWN (a satire against marriage) 1983

mixed media
238.8 x 167.6 x 12.7 cm
the artist
illustrated p. 90

14
WILLOW PATTERN 1984
mixed media
diameter 183 x 12.7 cm
the artist

BASIL BEATTIE
Born West Hartlepool 1935. Had four one-person exhibitions since 1979: at Newcastle Polytechnic Gallery; Goldsmiths' College of Art Gallery, London; The Minories, Colchester; and the Bede Gallery, Jarrow. Included in ten group exhibitions in the last few years, including the 6th Cleveland International Drawing Biennale.

15
OASIS 1983
acrylic and oil on cotton duck
213 x 306 cm
the artist

16
NORTH MARCH 1984
acrylic and oil on cotton duck
213 x 306 cm
the artist
illustrated p. 39

JOHN BELLANY
Born Port Seton, Scotland, 1942. Seventeen one-person exhibitions since 1979 in Britain, America and Australia. Inclusion in many mixed exhibitions in the last few years in Finland, Britain and Germany.
Monika Kinley, London

17
JANUS 1983
oil on canvas
172.7 x 122 cm
the artist
illustrated p. 126

18
PORTRAIT OF KEN KIFF 1984
oil on canvas
152.4 x 122 cm
the artist

19
THE SEVERED HEAD 1984
oil on canvas
172.7 x 152.4 cm
the artist

TONY BEVAN
Born Bradford 1951. Included in several mixed exhibitions since 1981, and had one-person exhibitions at Matt's Gallery, London; Galeria Akumulatory 2, Poznań Galerie Wittenbrink, Regensburg; and Chapter

Gallery, Cardiff. Selected
publications since 1982 include
Picture Book, 1982, and
Zeichnungen 1979–1984,
1984.
Matt's Gallery, London

20
BREAD AND COFFEE 1983
pigment and acrylic on canvas
184 x 162 cm
the artist
illustrated p. 131

21
THE HORIZON 1983–4
acrylic and pigment on canvas
256 x 180 cm
the artist

STUART BRISLEY
Born 1933. Since 1980 his work
has been seen in New York,
Canada, France, Holland,
Norway, Poland, Sweden and
West Germany as well as in
London, Edinburgh,
Birmingham, Exeter, Liverpool
and Newcastle.
Paul Johnstone, London

22
1 = 66,666 (GEORGIANA
COLLECTION VI) March 1983
wood, steel, plaster, leather,
nylon, cloth and paper
217 x 500 x 81 cm
Arts Council of Great Britain
illustrated p. 69

VICTOR BURGIN
Born Sheffield 1941. Editor of
Thinking Photography,
published by Macmilland, 1982.
His most recent work, 'The
Bridge', was shown at the John
Weber Gallery, New York, and
Liliane et Michel Durand-Dessert
Gallery, Paris, in 1984 and it will
be included in an exhibition of his
work at the ICA, London, in 1985.

23
GRADIVA 1982
A series of seven black and white
photographs
each 50.8 x 60.96 cm
the artist
illustrated p. 61

PAUL BUSH
Born London 1956. Member of
the London Film-makers Co-op
since 1978. Films shown in
London, Wales and New York as
part of mixed showings and one-
person events.

24
THE COW'S DRAMA 1983
16 mm film, 38 minutes, black
and white, magnetic sound
illustrated p. 101

STEVEN CAMPBELL
Born Glasgow 1954. Employed
as a steel works maintenance
engineer before taking a painting
degree from 1978 to 1982. Six
one-person exhibitions in New
York, Chicago, Munich and
London in 1983–4. Awarded
Fulbright Scholarship in 1982.

25
THE BUILDING ACCUSES
THE ARCHITECT OF BAD
DESIGN 1984
oil on canvas
287 x 287 cm
the artist
illustrated p. 89

ANTHONY CARO
Born New Malden, Surrey, 1924.
Sixteen one-person exhibitions in
Japan, Canada, America,
Britain, Germany and France
since 1979. In 1980 began to
make sculptures in lead, wood
and bronze. Appointed Trustee
of the Tate Gallery, and to the
Councils of the Slade School of
Art and the Royal College of Art.
Waddington & Knoedler
Galleries, London

26
AFTER EMMA 1977–82
steel, rusted, blacked and
painted
244 x 274 x 188 cm
Waddington and Knoedler
Galleries, London

27
BOMBAZINE 1980-2
brass and bronze, cast and
welded
87.6 x 92.7 x 63.5 cm
Waddington & Knoedler
Galleries, London
illustrated p. 99

JOHN CARTER
Born Middlesex 1942. Since
1979 had one-person exhibitions
at the University of Reading and
at Nicola Jacobs Gallery and the
Warwick Arts Trust, London.
Included in many mixed
exhibitions in the last few years.
Prize-winner in the Tolly Cobbold
Exhibition, 1981.
Nicola Jacobs Gallery, London

28
ASSEMBLY OF RECTANGLES
I – golden section, equal
areas 1981–2
oil on plywood
159 x 60 cm
the artist, courtesy Nicola Jacobs
Gallery, London

29
EQUAL AREAS WITHIN A

SQUARE – cadmium red and
deep cadmium 1983
oil on plywood
120 x 120 cm
the artist, courtesy Nicola Jacobs
Gallery, London
illustrated p. 46

TONY CARTER
Born West Riding of Yorkshire
1943. One-person exhibitions at
Anthony Stokes Gallery, London,
in 1979 and the Serpentine
Gallery, London, in 1983.
Included in mixed exhibitions in
Britain and America. Arts
Council Major Award given in
1980.

30
VIRUS – OF WAR AND
SUBJECTIVE SEEING 1979–82
oil paint over photographic print,
3 easels extended to approx.
228.5 cm, 1 chair
the artist
illustrated p. 80

31
PIETÀ 1982–3
relief in mixed media, including
postcard reproduction, bronze
casts, lead casts, rubber
mould, etc.
61.6 x 73 x 7 cm
the artist

HELEN CHADWICK
Born Croydon 1953. Selector of
part of 1979 Hayward Annual.
Involved in various artist
placement schemes, e.g. the
National Portrait Gallery,
London, and John Smith's
Brewery, Yorkshire. One-person
exhibitions since 1981 in
Newcastle, Sheffield, Brighton,
London, Derry, Belfast and
Portsmouth. Greater London Arts
Association Major Award in 1981
and Artist in Schools Award, from
Northern Arts, in 1983.

32
EGO GEOMETRIA SUM IX:
high school – age 13 1983
plywood and photographic
emulsion
70 x 70 x 70 cm
the artist
illustrated p. 117

33
EGO GEOMETRIA SUM:
the labours IX 1984
photograph from the series of 10
made in collaboration with Mark
Pilkington
94 x 125 cm
the artist

MARC CHAIMOWICZ
Born Paris 1945. One-person

exhibitions since 1979 in
London, Amsterdam, Vienna,
Lyons, Liverpool, Derry,
Southampton, Leeds, Geneva
and Dijon. One of four artists in
the Arts Council 1983–4 touring
exhibition 'Four Rooms'.
Performances of 'Doubts' and
'Partial Eclipse' given since 1979
in New York, Amsterdam,
Munich, London and Vienna.
Nigel Greenwood Inc., London

34
SUMMER DIPTYCH, LEANING
. . . WITH CHORUS GIRLS
AND SENTINELS London 1984
2 glass panels, 5 wood panels,
photographs, oil medium, gloss
paint
183 x 335 cm approx.
the artist, courtesy Nigel
Greenwood Inc.

ALAN CHARLTON
Born Sheffield 1948. One-
person exhibitions since 1979 in
Düsseldorf, Amsterdam,
Eindhoven, London, Paris,
Edinburgh, Zürich, Brussels.
Included in several mixed
exhibitions recently, e.g. 'The
New Spirit in Painting', London,
1981, and 'Documenta 7',
Kassel, in 1982.

35
THREE PANEL PAINTING 1982
acrylic on cotton duck
each panel 250 x 125 cm
Konrad Fischer Gallery,
Düsseldorf

TONY CRAGG
Born Liverpool 1949. Since 1977
living in Germany and from 1979
teaching at the Düsseldorf
Kunstakademie. Forty-two one-
person exhibitions since 1979 in
London, Berlin, Hamburg,
Bristol, Düsseldorf, Paris,
Naples, Milan, Genoa, Munich,
St Etienne, Lyons, Wuppertal,
Karlsruhe, Tokyo, New York,
Otterlo, Amsterdam, Berne, Rio
de Janeiro, St Gallen, Toronto,
Middleburg and Lousiana,
Denmark.
Lisson Gallery, London

36
OPENING SPIRAL 1982
mixed media – found objects
152 x 408 x 152 cm
Lisson Gallery, London
illustrated p. 104

37
DRY PLACE 1984
wood, metal, wax crayon
290 x 150 x 150 cm
the artist, courtesy Lisson
Gallery, London

MICHAEL CRAIG-MARTIN
Born Dublin 1941. Nine one-person exhibitions since 1978 in Warsaw, Poznań, Dublin, London, Paris and New York. Participated in group exhibitions organized by the British Council for India and Japan. Commission from the Midland Bank, New York, in 1983.
Waddington Galleries Ltd, London

38
TOWER 1981
tape on wall
dimensions to be determined in situ
the artist, courtesy Waddington Galleries, London

39
SHARP PRACTICE 1984
oil on aluminium panels with painted steel lines
91.4 x 213.4 x 25.4 cm (approx.)
the artist, courtesy Waddington Galleries, London
illustrated p. 105

JOHN DAVIES
Born Cheshire 1946. One-person exhibitions held at Marlborough Fine Art, London, in 1980 and 1984; Kunstverein, Hamburg, and tour 1981; and Ferens Art Gallery, Hull, in 1983. Participation in many group exhibitions in Europe, Australia and South America since 1979.
Marlborough Fine Art (London) Ltd

40
HEAD OF D.R. 1981–3
mixed media
height 29.9 cm
private collection

41
FIGURE AND WIRE MESH 1982–3
pastel, crayon and pencil
211 x 61 cm
Marlborough Fine Art (London) Ltd

42
S.H. LINED FACE 1982–3
mixed media
height 43.2 cm
Marlborough Fine Art (London) Ltd

43
HEAD 1983
plaster, epoxy resin and mixed media
19 x 11.4 x 13.3 cm
Tony Reichardt

44
HEAD OF P.W. 1983
mixed media

height 32 cm
collection of Richard Salmon

45
HEAD OF B.N. 1981–4
mixed media
height 30.5 cm
Marlborough Fine Art (London) Ltd

RICHARD DEACON
Born in Wales 1949. One-person exhibitions since 1980 at The Gallery, Acre Lane, London; Sheffield Polytechnic Gallery; Lisson Gallery, London; Orchard Gallery, Derry; Riverside Studios, London; and Chapter Arts Centre, Cardiff. In 1982 selector for the sculpture section of the New Contemporaries show. Included in twenty-one group exhibitions since 1980.
Lisson Gallery, London

46
UNTITLED 1980
galvanized sheet steel
125 x 345 x 125 cm
the artist, courtesy Lisson Gallery, London

47
OUT OF THE HOUSE 1983
galvanized steel and linoleum with rivets
122 x 61 x 152.5 cm
Saatchi Collection, London

48
THE EYE HAS IT 1984
wood, galvanized steel, stainless steel, brass and cloth
80 x 345 x 170 cm
Arts Council of Great Britain
illustrated p. 44

GRAHAM DURWARD
Born Aberdeen 1956. One-person exhibitions at the 369 Gallery, Edinburgh, in 1979, 1981 and 1983, and the Friejus/Ordorer Gallery, New York, in 1984. Included in several mixed exhibitions since 1981 in Scotland, America and London.
369 Gallery, Edinburgh

49
FIRST CRIME IN THE FOREST 1984
oil on canvas
198 x 319 cm
the artist
illustrated p. 68

50
SCREWING THE EARTH 1984
oil on canvas
198 x 334 cm
the artist

IAN HAMILTON FINLAY
Born Nassau, Bahamas, 1925.

Has outdoor sculptures sited at the Kröller-Müller Museum, Otterlo; the Max Planck Institute, Stuttgart; and in other European gardens. Lives in Little Sparta, on the Lanarkshire moors, where he develops his garden. Recently conducting Little Sparta's War with Strathclyde Region over the question of rates, and commanded the Saint-Just Vigilantes at The First Battle of Little Sparta in 1983.
Graeme Murray Gallery, Edinburgh

51
INSCRIPTION 1984
made in collaboration with Michael Harvey
nebrasina
41.6 x 38 x 5 cm
the artist

ROSE FINN-KELCEY
Born 1940. Important shows in which she has participated in the last five years include 'About Time', ICA Gallery, London, 1980; 'London/LA' in New York, 1981; and the International Festival of Performance Art, Lyons, in 1982. Recent performances have been given at Matt's Gallery and the Royal College of Art Gallery, London.

52
GLORY 1983
colour videotape, 20 minutes
illustrated p. 72

53
ELEVATION 1984
repeated performance

GARETH FISHER
Born Penrith, 1951. Included in recent mixed exhibitions in Edinburgh, New York, Nova Scotia, Newcastle, Glasgow and London. One-person exhibitions in Edinburgh, 1978, and Toronto, 1984. Chairman of the New 57 Gallery, Edinburgh, from 1979 to 1981.

54
SPROUTING HEAD 1983
plaster and mixed media
45.7 x 25.4 x 25.4 cm
the artist
illustrated p. 92

55
FLAG 1984
plaster and mixed media
213.4 x 91.4 x 91.4 cm
the artist

56
UNTITLED 1984
plaster and mixed media
101.6 x 46 x 46 cm
the artist

JOEL FISHER
Born Salem, Ohio, 1947. Twelve one-person exhibitions in Britain and Europe since 1979. Included in several group exhibitions in Italy, America, Britain, Poland, Belgium and France in the last few years. Two publications of 1984 are *A Second Furlong*, Matt's Gallery, London, and *Zwischen zwei und drei Dimensionen/Between two and three Dimensions*, Kunstmuseum, Luzern.
Nigel Greenwood Inc., London

57
CAVE 1983
bronze
12 x 23 x 17 cm
the artist, courtesy NIgel Greenwood Inc.

58
Apograph for CAVE 1983
conté crayon on handmade paper
15 x 15 cm
the artist, courtesy Nigel Greenwood Inc.

59
PAPABILUS 1982–4
bronze
58 x 66 x 48 cm
the artist, courtesy Nigel Greenwood Inc.
illustrated p. 107

60
Apograph for PAPABILUS 1982
conté crayon on handmade paper
15 x 15 cm
private collection
illustrated p. 107

BARRY FLANAGAN
Born Prestatyn, North Wales 1941. Fourteen one-person exhibitions in Europe and America since 1979, which include the British Council entry to the 1982 Venice Biennale. Participation in several group exhibitions in Europe and Japan. Subject of a South Bank Television show, 1984.
Waddington Galleries, London

61
HARE AND HELMET III 1981
bronze
height 117 cm
private collection

62
SOPRANO bronze No. 7 1981
bronze, partly gilded
80 x 66 x 57 cm
Arts Council of Great Britain
illustrated p. 83

GILBERT & GEORGE
Gilbert – born Dolomites, Italy, 1943. George – born Devon 1942. Twenty one (two)-person exhibitions in Europe and America since 1979. An Arts Council film, *The World of Gilbert & George*, made in 1981. Included in twenty-eight group exhibitions since 1978.
Anthony d'Offay Gallery, London

63
BLOODED 1983
photo-piece
302.5 x 252.5 cm
Anthony d'Offay Gallery, London
illustrated p. 115

SANDRA GOLDBACHER
Born London 1960. Completed postgraduate year in Film and Video at Middlesex Polytechnic in 1983. Included in the 1984 Anglo-French Video Exchange shown both at the Tate Gallery, London, and the Pompidou Centre, Paris, and the Anglo-Canadian Video Exchange shown in Toronto and London. Works in collaboration with the video artist Kim Flitcroft.

64
POLKA DOTS AND MOONBEAMS 1983
colour videotape, 13½ minutes
illustrated p. 120

ANTONY GORMLEY
Born London 1950. One-person exhibitions at the Whitechapel Gallery and the Serpentine Gallery, London, 1981; Coracle Press, London, 1983; and Salvatore Ala Gallery, New York, in 1984. Included in British Council touring exhibition 'Transformations', which was shown in South America and Portugal 1983-4.
Salvatore Ala Gallery, New York and Milan

65
THREE BODIES 1981
lead, fibreglass and earth
Rock: 96 x 60 x 54 cm;
Shark: 18 x 193 x 60 cm;
Pumpkin: 50 x 50 x 44 cm
the artist, courtesy Salvatore Ala Gallery, New York

MICK HARTNEY
Born London 1946. Included in several group exhibitions in the last few years, including a British Council touring show in Japan and the Anglo-Canadian Video Exchange, Toronto and London.

66
DICKLER'S WHAMMY – a fiction 1982-3

colour videotape 17 minutes
stereo sound
illustrated p. 114

TIM HEAD
Born London 1946. Nine one-person exhibitions since 1979 in Brisbane, Milan, London, Glasgow, Paris, Genoa and Hasselt, and the British Pavilion in the 1980 Venice Biennale. Included in twenty group exhibitions since 1979 in Europe, Australia and America. In 1984 commissioned to do an outdoor piece by the National Museum of Photography, Film and Television, Bradford.
Juda Rowan Gallery, London

67
STATE OF THE ART 1984
colour photograph
183 x 274 cm
the artist
illustrated p. 60

GERARD HEMSWORTH
Born London 1945. Fourteen one-person exhibitions since 1979 in Dublin, Derry, Poznań, Berlin, Antwerp, Bremerhaven, Cambridge, London, Kraków, Nottingham and Glasgow. Included in several group exhibitions in Europe in the last few years.
Anthony Reynolds, London

68
DELUGE 1983
acrylic on canvas
244 x 153 cm
the artist, courtesy Anthony Reynolds
illustrated p. 118

69
ECLIPSE 1983
acrylic on canvas
244 x 305 cm
the artist, courtesy Anthony Reynolds

SUSAN HILLER
Born America 1940. Twenty-two one-person exhibitions in Europe, Canada and Australia since 1978, in which recent large works such as 'Monument', 'Elan' and 'Belshazzar's Feast/The Writing on the Wall' have been included. Recent publications are *The Muse My Sister* published by the Orchard Gallery, Derry, and *Sisters of Menon*, by the Coracle Press, London.
Gimpel Fils, London

70a
AUTOBIOGRAPHY 1982
liquid silver leaf on photograph, dry-mounted on linen

233 x 137 cm
the artist

70b
SELF PORTRAIT 1983
liquid metalic leaf on photograph, dry-mounted on linen
233 x 137 cm
the artist

71
MIDNIGHT, BAKER STREET 1983
set of 3 C-type photographs, enlarged from hand-coloured automatic photographs
each 71 x 51 cm
Arts Council of Great Britain
illustrated p. 106

JOHN HILLIARD
Born Lancaster 1945. Since 1978 had eleven one-person exhibitions in Birmingham, Warsaw, Paris, London, Stuttgart, Derry, Osaka, Kyoto and Cambridge. Most recent publication is *Borderland*, published by the Orchard Gallery, Derry, in 1981. Included in many mixed exhibitions in Europe, America and Japan in the last few years.

72
FAÇADE 1982
cibachromes on gaterfoam
80 x 200 cm
the artist

73
MASQUERADE 1982
cibachromes on aluminium
80 x 200 cm
the artist
illustrated p. 112

HOWARD HODGKIN
Born London 1932. Thirteen one-person exhibitions since 1979, which includes the show 'Forty Paintings 1973–84' presented at the British Pavilion, 1984 Venice Biennale, and touring on to Washington, New Haven, Hannover and London. Included in numerous mixed exhibitions since 1979. In 1981 was the subject of a South Bank Show television programme, and in 1982 an Arts Council film was made about his work.
M. Knoedler and Co. Inc., New York

74
LAWSON, UNDERWOOD AND SLEEP 1977-80
oil on wood
61 x 91.4 cm
private collection

75
SOUVENIR 1981

original screenprint on arches aquarelle mould-made paper
114.3 x 139.7 cm
Petersburg Press Ltd
illustrated p. 36

SHIRAZEH HOUSHIARY
Born Iran 1955. Junior Fellow in Fine Art, Cardiff College of Art, 1979–80. One-person exhibitions since 1980 at Chapter Arts Centre, Cardiff; Kettle's Yard, Cambridge, 1982; and in 1983 at Centro d'arte Contemporanea, Siracusa; Massimo Minini Gallery, Milan; and Grita Insam Gallery, Vienna. Included in fifteen group exhibitions since 1982.
Lisson Gallery, London

76
FIRE STOLEN BY BIRD 1981
7 objects: clay and wood
varying heights:
from 61 to 137 cm
the artist, courtesy Lisson Gallery, London
illustrated p. 45

77
CRESCENT OF THE EARTH 1983
wire, plaster, clay, straw
163.9 x 251.5 x 50.8 cm
the artist, courtesy Lisson Gallery, London

ANTHONY HOWELL
Born London 1945. In 1981 decided to go solo from The Ting: Theatre of Mistakes, which he founded in 1974. Since 1981 performed in Belgium, Amsterdam, the Performance Festival, Berlin, and the 1982 Sydney Biennale. Artist in Residence at Sydney College of the Arts, 1983–4. Recent works include 'The Tower' and 'The Life Class'.

78
TABLE MOVE II
performance, 36 minutes
first performed 1981
illustrated p. 102

79
TABLE MOVE I
performance, 36 minutes
first performed 1983

JOHN HOYLAND
Born Sheffield 1934. In 1979 was Artist in Residence at Melbourne University and in 1980 selected the Hayward Annual for the Arts Council. Fifteen one-person exhibitions since 1979 in America, Britain, Australia and Europe. In 1983 awarded first prize at the John Moores exhibition, Liverpool.

Waddington Galleries Ltd,
London

80
WIZARD 14.10.1983
acrylic on canvas
243.8 x 228.6 cm
Waddington Galleries, London
illustrated p. 38

81
ZLAR 10.10.1983
acrylic on canvas
243.8 x 228.6 cm
Waddington Galleries, London

JOHN HYATT
Born Leeds 1958. Attended
Leeds University. From 1982
part-time teaching in Leeds and
Rochdale, and formed a band,
The Three Johns, with John
Brennan and John Langford.
One-person exhibition at
Rochdale Art Gallery in 1984.

82
ART, WARS, DIVISION AND
DESIGN June–August 1982
oil, housepaint and carspray on
canvas
124.5 x 266.7 cm
the artist
illustrated p. 62 and cover

83
ZEITGEIST OR TREE OF
MODERN ART OR PIGS
MIGHT FLY January 1984
oil on canvas
61 x 91.4 cm
the artist

STEPHEN JOHNSON
Born Whitstable 1953. Post-
graduate year at Chelsea School
of Art 1981–2. Included in eight
group exhibitions in London
since 1980.

84
CLOUD 1982
plated copper
7.6 cm high
the artist
illustrated p. 85

85
WISH FULFILMENT 1982
patinated cupro nickel
width 178 cm
the artist

86
STICKS MINUS PHOSPHORUS
(EXORCISM) 1983
wood and paper
height 274 cm
the artist

PETER JOSEPH
Born 1929. Awarded prize at the
John Moores Exhibition,
Liverpool, in 1979. Eight one-

person exhibitions since 1979 in
Paris, Düsseldorf, London, Basle
and Chicago. Included in several
group exhibitions in the last few
years.
Lisson Gallery, London

87
ROSE WITH BROWN
SURROUND February 1983
acrylic on cotton duck
157 x 153 cm
the artist
illustrated p. 51

88
DARK GREY CENTRE WITH
DARK BLUE
SURROUND August 1983
acrylic on cotton duck
178 x 152.4 cm
the artist

ANISH KAPOOR
Born Bombay, India, 1954. Nine
one-person exhibitions since
1980 in Paris, London,
Rotterdam, Liverpool, Lyons and
New York. Has participated in
several mixed exhibitions,
including the Aperto section of
the 1982 Venice Biennale and
the British Council touring show
'Transformations' in 1983–4,
which visited South America and
Portugal.
Lisson Gallery, London

89
1,000 NAMES 1980
wood, pigment
overall size 17 x 233 x 127 cm
the artist, courtesy Lisson
Gallery, London

90
UNTITLED 1983
cement, gesso, pigment and
polystyrene
160 x 106 x 106 cm
the artist, courtesy Lisson
Gallery, London

MARY KELLY
Born America 1941. In 1983 the
complete 'Post-Partum
Document' was presented in
book form, published by
Routledge & Kegan Paul. Since
1976 this work has been
exhibited in Britain, Europe,
Australia, Canada and America.

91
POST-PARTUM DOCUMENT
DOCUMENTATION VI
pre-writing alphabet, exergue
and diary 1979
resin and slate
15 units 20.3 x 25.4 cm
Arts Council of Great Britain
illustrated p. 100

KEN KIFF
Born Dagenham 1935. Eight
one-person exhibitions since
1979 in Brighton, London,
Edinburgh, Stirling, Dundee and
New York. Included in twenty
mixed exhibitions since 1979 in
Britain, America, Australia and
Europe.
Nicola Jacobs Gallery, London

92
GUSHING STREAM
SEQUENCE 130 1978–9
acrylic on paper
58.4 x 73.7 cm
the artist, courtesy Nicola Jacobs
Gallery, London

93
THE FEMININE AS GENEROUS,
FRIGHTENING AND
SERENE 1982–3
oil on canvas
160 x 129.5 cm
the artist, courtesy Nicola Jacobs
Gallery, London
illustrated p. 130

R. B. KITAJ
Born Cleveland, Ohio, 1932. In
1979 returned to London after a
period in New York. In same year
first New York exhibition of
pastels and drawings. 1980
organized one of 'The Artist's
Eye' series at the National
Gallery, London. In 1982 elected
to American Institute of Arts and
Letters and awarded Honorary
Doctorate from University
College, London.
Malborough Fine Art
(London) Ltd

94
CECIL COURT, LONDON WC2
(the refugees) 1983–4
oil on canvas
182.9 x 182.9 cm
the artist, courtesy Marlborough
Fine Art (London) Ltd
illustrated p. 32

LEON KOSSOFF
Born London 1926. Since 1979
had one-person exhibitions at
Fischer Fine Art and the
Riverside Studios, London;
Museum of Modern Art, Oxford;
L. A. Louver Gallery, Los Angeles;
and Hirsch and Adler Modern
Gallery, New York.
Fischer Fine Art, London

95
SELF PORTRAIT 1980
oil on board
24 x 21.3 cm
private collection

96
FIDELMA IN A RED
CHAIR 1982
oil on board
62.2 x 48.2 cm
private collection
illustrated p. 34

97
FAMILY PARTY,
JANUARY 1983 1983
oil on board
167.6 x 249.5 cm
Saatchi Collection, London

BOB LAW
Born London 1934. Had four
one-person exhibitions since his
Whitechapel Gallery
retrospective in 1978; Galerie
Nancy Gillespie – Elizabeth De
Laage, Paris, 1979; Lisson
Gallery, London, in 1980 and
1982; and Gunnersbury Park,
London, also in 1982. Since
1980 Law has turned to
sculpture.
Lisson Gallery, London

98
INSTALLATION
a
CAST BLACK DIAMOND 1980
iron
21 x 23 cm
the artist
b
HOLE WITHIN A WHOLE 1980
iron
161 x 15 x 46 cm
the artist
c
PLUTO 1980
iron
2.6 x 3.8 x 3 cm
the artist
d
WAY 1980
iron
10 x 18.5 x 23 cm
the artist
e
UNTITLED 1980–4
bronze
16 x 8.5 x 8 cm
the artist
f
BALLS WITH OBELISK 1963-
84
bronze
12.5 x 29 x 8.5 cm overall
the artist

99
HOLE WITHIN WHOLE,
ON WHEELS 1984
bronze 1/2 edition
27 x 38 x 23 cm
the artist

100
VINCENT'S CHAIR 1984
painted wood

90 x 46 x 45 cm
the artist
illustrated p. 52

RICHARD LONG
Born Bristol 1945. Since 1979
had forty-one one-person
exhibitions in Japan, Europe and
North America. Works made in
Morocco, Mexico, Bolivia,
Iceland, Nepal, Lapland,
Barbados and India.
Anthony d'Offay Gallery, London

101
SEA LEVEL WATER LINE
Death Valley California 1982
one frame
124 x 88 cm
Anthony d'Offay Gallery, London

102
THREE MOORS THREE
CIRCLES 1982
printed work
103 x 153 cm
Anthony d'Offay Gallery, London
illustrated p. 103

103
WINTER CIRCLE 1984
30 stones of Cornish slate
diameter 160 cm
Anthony d'Offay Gallery, London

LEONARD McCOMB
Born Glasgow 1930. In 1983
resumed painting in oil after
abandoning it in 1980. One-
person exhibitions at Coracle
Press, London, in 1979 and the
Serpentine Gallery, London, in
1983, which toured to Oxford,
Manchester, Brighton and
Edinburgh.

104
ROCK AND SEA,
ANGLESEY 1983
pencil, watercolour and ink on
handmade paper
457.5 x 457.5 cm
the artist
illustrated p. 37

105
BOWL 1984
polished bronze
57 cm diameter x 36 cm high
the artist

106
SPRING FLOWERS,
ANGLESEY 1984
4 pen and ink drawings on
handmade paper
the artist
a
BLOSSOMS OVER THE SEA
15.5 x 24 cm
b
DAFFODILS OVERLOOKING
THE SEA
15 x 24 cm

c
PRIMROSES
15 x 24 cm
d
WOOD ANEMONES IN GLASS
24.5 x 14.5 cm

JOCK McFADYEN
Born Paisley 1950. One-person
exhibitions since 1979 at the
Acme Gallery, London; Hull
College of Higher Education;
Bede Gallery, Jarrow; St Paul's
Gallery, Leeds; Compass Gallery,
Glasgow; and Blond Fine Art,
London. Arts Council Major
Award in 1979 and Artist in
Residence at the National
Gallery, London, in 1981.
Blond Fine Art, London

107
PORTRAIT OF IAN PAISLEY:
'YOU CAN KNOCK ME DOWN,
STEAL MY CAR, DRINK MY
LIQUOR FROM AN OLD
FRUIT JAR, BUT
DON'TCHA . . .' 1981
oil on card
137.2 x 101.6 cm
the artist
illustrated p. 66

108
LEGEND OF THE WOLF III
1983
oil on card
132.1 x 97.8 cm
the artist

109
STILL LIFE WITH
UNION JACK 1983
oil on card
132.1 x 97.8 cm
the artist

IAN McKEEVER
Born Withernsea, East Yorkshire,
1946. Eleven one-person
exhibitions since 1979 in
London, Bristol, Glasgow,
Liverpool, Oxford, Nürnberg and
Munich. Artist in Residence at
the Bridewell Studios, Liverpool,
in 1980–1 and in Nürnberg in
1981-2. Subject of an Audio Arts
cassette in 1982.
Nigel Greenwood Inc., London

110
NIGHT FLAK 1980–1
oil on canvas/charcoal and pastel
on paper
2 panels each 213 x 152 cm
Nigel Greenwood Inc.

111
BESIDE THE BRAMBLED
DITCH 1983
oil on photograph on canvas
230 x 208 cm
Collection of the Contemporary

Art Society (Linbury Trust
Donation)
illustrated p. 82

STEPHEN McKENNA
Born London 1939. Eleven one-
person exhibitions since 1979 in
London, Gent, Washington,
Belfast, Derry, Antwerp,
Brussels, Oxford, Berlin and
Eindhoven. Participated in
several group exhibitions in the
last few years including both
'New Art' and 'The Hard Won
Image' at the Tate Gallery,
London.

112
O, ILIUM! 1982
oil on canvas
180 x 250 cm
Galerie Isy Brachot,
Brussels-Paris
illustrated p. 58

113
SELINUNTE 1983
oil on canvas
150 x 250 cm
the artist

BRUCE McLEAN
Born Glasgow 1944. Since 1979
had twenty-six one-person
exhibitions in Southampton,
London, Zürich, Glasgow,
Edinburgh, Bristol, Paris,
St-Etienne, Amsterdam, Basle,
Vienna, Tokyo, New York,
Eindhoven, Düsseldorf, Berlin,
Munich, Florence and Karlsruhe.
Awarded DAAD Fellowship,
Berlin, in 1981.
Anthony d'Offay Gallery, London

114
SCOTTISH HAT AND SWORD
DANCE 1982
acrylic and chalk on cotton
3 parts, each: 280 x 150 cm
overall size: 280 x 450 cm
Anthony d'Offay Gallery, London
illustrated p. 59

ALASTAIR MacLENNAN
Born Scotland 1943. Lived in
Belfast since 1975. Since 1979
given performances in London,
Derry, Dublin, Cork, Belfast,
Edinburgh, Quebec, Poznań,
Wrocław, St Andrews, Berlin,
San Francisco, Glasgow, Leeds,
Coimbra, Novoli, Toronto,
Calgary, Vancouver, Los
Angeles, New York, Brighton,
Dartington, Fribourg, Turin,
Liverpool, Chicago and Seattle.

115
FOUR RELATED
PERFORMANCE-
INSTALLATIONS
1984-5

a
BURIED ALIVE
24-hour non-stop work
b
IF UNDERHAND
40-hour non-stop work
c
BODY BREAK
72-hour non-stop work
d
LIES IN WEIGHT
96-hour non-stop work

KENNETH MARTIN
Born Sheffield 1905. Since
1979, and his retrospective show
at the Yale Center for British Art,
New Haven, had eleven one-
person exhibitions in Montreal,
Bochum, New York, London,
Bern, Leicester, Stockholm,
Helsinki, Malmö and The Hague.
Waddington Galleries, London

116
CHANCE ORDER CHANGE 25,
HISTORY PAINTING B 1982
oil on canvas
91.4 x 91.4 cm
Waddington Galleries, London

117
CHANCE ORDER CHANGE 27,
HISTORY PAINTING 1983
oil on canvas
91.4 x 116.5 cm
Waddington Galleries, London
illustrated p. 98

JOHN MURPHY
Born St Albans 1945. Eight one-
person exhibitions since 1979 in
London, Melbourne, Warsaw,
Belfast, Derry and Gent.
Included in mixed exhibitions
since 1979 in Gent, Deurle,
Stuttgart, Bern, London,
Wrocław and Venice.
Lisson Gallery, London

118
THE SKELETON AT THE FEAST
. . . A SPECTRE IS HAUNTING
EUROPE 1982
oil on linen
198 x 168 cm
the artist, courtesy Lisson
Gallery, London

119
THE GATHERING ANGUISH
STRIKES BENEATH 1982–3
oil on linen
185.4 x 144.8 cm
private collection
illustrated p. 81

AVIS NEWMAN
Born London 1946. One-person
exhibitions at Matt's Gallery,
London, and the Ikon Gallery,
Birmingham, both in 1982.
Included in several mixed

drawing exhibitions since 1979, including the 1982 Hayward Annual and in mixed gallery show at Serpentine Gallery, London, 1984.
Matt's Gallery, London

120
THIS . . . THE DREAM'S NAVEL 1983-4
two-part piece:
mixed media on canvas
274.3 x 366 cm
boxed book – steel box and lithograph on paper
50.8 x 39.4 cm
the artist
illustrated p. 49

GERALD NEWMAN
Born Marlborough 1945. One-person exhibitions at the ICA Gallery, London, and the Ikon Gallery, Birmingham, in 1981, Matt's Gallery, London, 1982, and De Appel/Radio Hilversum, Amsterdam, 1983. Participated in mixed exhibitions in recent years, including the 1982 Sydney Biennale and British Soundworks at Franklin Furnace, New York.
Anthony Reynolds, London

121
SOUTH ATLANTIC 1982
(Times nos. 14 & 15)
stereophonic tape recording
28 min
Imperial War Museum
represented p. 72

PHILIP NICOL
Born Caerphilly 1953. From 1979 to 1984 teaching in art colleges in Cardiff, Winchester, Birmingham, Leeds, Chelsea and Limerick. Included in recent years in mixed exhibitions in Birmingham, Cardiff, Stuttgart, Aberystwyth, London and Limerick. Artist in Residence in Stuttgart, 1984.

122
DOUBLE-TAKE 1982
acrylic on cotton duck
305 x 366 cm
the artist
illustrated p. 134

123
BELLY-UP No. 2 1983
acrylic on cotton duck
213.4 x 211 cm
the artist

THÉRÈSE OULTON
Born Shrewsbury 1953. Post-graduate year at the Royal College of Art, 1983. One-person exhibition at Gimpel Fils, London, 1984. Artist in

Residence at Winchester School of Art, 1983–4. Included in nine mixed exhibitions since 1982.
Gimpel Fils, London

124
SPACE FOR LEDA 1983
oil on canvas
269 x 228.5 cm
the artist, courtesy Gimpel Fils

125
OLD GOLD 1984
oil on canvas
205.7 x 259.1 cm
Frankel Collection, Philadelphia, USA
illustrated p. 87

JAYNE PARKER
Born Nottingham 1957. Post-graduate work at the Slade School of Art 1980–2, Video Fellowship at North East London Polytechnic, 1983–4. Films screened in Britain, Europe and America.

126
I DISH 1982
16 mm film, 16 minutes, black and white, magnetic sound
illustrated p. 132

PAULA REGO
Born Lisbon, Portugal, 1935. Eight one-person exhibitions since 1979 in London, Lisbon, Amsterdam, Bristol, Milan and Nottingham. Included in many mixed exhibitions since 1979 in Paris, Nottingham, London, Liverpool, Baden-Baden, New York and Penzance.
Edward Totah Gallery, London

127
LA BOHÈME 1983
acrylic on paper
240 x 203 cm
the artist, courtesy Edward Totah Gallery
illustrated p. 127

128
GENUFA 1983
acrylic on paper
240 x 203 cm
the artist, courtesy Edward Totah Gallery

MICHAEL SANDLE
Born Weymouth 1936. Professorships of Fine Art in Pforzheim 1977-80, and in Karlsruhe, 1980. Elected member of the Royal Academy, London, 1982. Recent one-person exhibitions held at Galerie Suzanne Fischer, Baden-Baden, 1979; Fischer Fine Art, London, 1981; and Kunstverein, Mannheim, in 1983.
Fischer Fine Art, London

129
SECOND WORLD WAR MEMORIAL 1981
bronze, edition of 8
55 x 134 x 72 cm
Fischer Fine Art, London
illustrated p. 93

TERRY SETCH
Born London 1936. Six one-person exhibitions since 1979 in Cardiff, London, Vancouver, Bristol and Melbourne, Australia. Artist in Residence, Victorian College of Arts, Melbourne, in 1983. Elected to the Faculty of Painting, British School in Rome, 1984.
Nigel Greenwood Inc., London

130
TWO WOMEN, GREENHAM June 1984
encaustic wax and oil on canvas
305 x 351 cm
the artist, courtesy Nigel Greenwood Inc.
illustrated p. 70

131
PEOPLE – stand together August 1984
encaustic wax and oil on canvas
274 x 437 cm
the artist, courtesy Nigel Greenwood Inc.

JOHN SMITH
Born London 1952. Films screened since 1979 at film festivals in Edinburgh, Berlin, London and Paris. Included in mixed touring exhibitions since 1978 in Britain and North America. Films shown on Thames and BBC Television.

132
SHEPHERD'S DELIGHT 1980-4
16 mm film, 36 minutes, colour, sound
illustrated p. 113

RAY SMITH
Born Harrow 1949. Four one-person exhibitions since 1980 at the Mostyn Art Gallery, Llandudno, the Ikon Gallery, Birmingham, and the ICA Gallery, London, all in 1980, and the John Hansard Gallery, Southampton, in 1982. Included in mixed exhibitions in recent years in Britain and Europe.

133
THE YOUNG BATHER 1982
acrylic on canvas
152.4 x 213.4 cm
the artist
illustrated p. 116

134
EMILY TAKES THE STAGE 1983
acrylic on canvas
106 x 153 cm
the artist

STATION HOUSE OPERA
Founded 1980. Based in London. Since 1981 performances given at the Symposium International d'Art Performance, Lyons; Mickery Theatre, Amsterdam; Waterloo Studios, London; Brooklyn Bridge Centenary, New York; ICA Theatre, London; and the South Bank, London.

135
SEX & DEATH 1981–2
performance, 35 minutes

ANDREW WALKER
Born Aberdeen 1959. Graduated from Edinburgh College of Art in 1981. Included in mixed exhibitions in Edinburgh and Glasgow since 1982. One-person exhibition at the Henderson Gallery, Edinburgh, 1982.

136
ANGEL AND BLUE CAT June 1982
oil on canvas
114.3 x 91.4 cm
the artist
illustrated p. 135

137
FAUNA & FLORA March 1983
oil on canvas
152.4 x 114.3 cm
the artist

138
HELL'S GATE September 1983
oil on canvas
167.6 x 244 cm
the artist

JOHN WALKER
Born Birmingham 1939. Nine one-person exhibitions since 1979 in New York, Melbourne, Australia, London, Washington, Louisville and Brookline. Guggenheim Fellow, 1981-2. Artist in Residence, Prahran, Melbourne, 1980. At present Dean, Victorian College of the Arts, Melbourne, Australia.
Nigel Greenwood Inc., London

139
OCEANIA MY DILEMMA II (triptych) 1983–4
oil on canvas
215.9 x 508 cm
the artist, courtesy M. Knoedler & Co. Inc., New York
illustrated p. 128